For Sale by Owner

6th EDITION

For Sale by Owner

6th EDITION

ROBERT IRWIN

PUBLISHING

New York

This publication is designed to provide accurate and authoritative information in regard to the subject matter covered. It is sold with the understanding that neither the author nor the publisher are not engaged in rendering legal, accounting, or other professional service. If legal advice or other expert assistance is required, the services of a competent professional should be sought.

The reader is advised that some of the websites noted in this book may have changed location since the book was printed while others may no longer exist. The publisher and the author do not endorse nor guarantee any of the services or products offered by websites mention in this book.

Published by Kaplan Publishing, a division of Kaplan, Inc.
1 Liberty Plaza, 24th Floor
New York, NY 10006

Printed in the United States of America

June 2008
10 9 8 7 6 5 4 3 2 1

ISBN-13: 978-1-4277-9746-9

Kaplan Publishing books are available at special quantity discounts to use for sales promotions, employee premiums, or educational purposes. Please email our Special Sales Department to order or for more information at *kaplanpublishing@kaplan.com* or write to Kaplan Publishing, 1 Liberty Plaza, 24th Floor, New York, NY 10006.

Contents

Foreword

AS CEO OF *Owners.com*, America's largest for-sale-by-owner market, I've seen hundreds of FSBO tools and services established over the last few years. As a result, I'm firmly committed to selling by owner.

My own real estate career began at age 18 when I used my college tuition as a down payment to purchase a $47,000 house in Ohio. At the time, I found the homebuying process frustrating with limited access to information on home listings, property values, and financing. Back then I was forced to work with real estate agents just to find out listing prices! To make matters worse, I felt real estate agents were not looking out for my best interests. Instead of showing me homes that truly fit my needs, I felt they were often steering me towards properties that would pay them the highest commissions. After encountering all of these problems and paying expensive real estate commissions, I became driven to find a better and less expensive way to buy and sell real estate.

I saw an opportunity to make a difference in the real estate market when I later joined Owners.com. The Internet could clearly make buying and selling homes easier and less expensive. Companies such as Owners.com made it possible for homeowners to reach prospective buyers in their local neighborhood directly through an online marketplace.

That Internet marketplace has matured due to the work of our company and others. For example, Owners.com helped pioneer new strategies such as "Flat Fee MLS" whereby a seller now can list on the Multiple Listing Service for a flat fee, currently just $377. We've added other services to help buyers and sellers obtain financing for homes they find on Owners.com, while title companies assist sellers with the closing process.

The for-sale-by-owner market has evolved significantly over the past decade. No longer are owners limited to newspaper ads and generic signs to market their homes.

Today's FSBO is not alone; a new industry has formed to help owners sell their properties for top dollar without paying commission.

While researching the FSBO market I discovered *For Sale by Owner* and was impressed by how well it explains selling by owner. Not only does it provide practical marketing advice, it also sets a realistic expectation of what it takes to successfully sell without using an agent.

I contacted the author, Robert Irwin, and eventually asked him to create a video, which can currently be seen on Owners.com, explaining the FSBO process. Our discussions ultimately led to including *For Sale by Owner* on *Owners.com*. We realized that it would make a complete by-owner selling solution. This latest edition of *For Sale By Owner* provides all of the know-how, tools, and services you will need to successfully market your home.

I am pleased to write this Foreward and to help you sell your property. I commend you for your decision to take control of your future.

Steve Udelson, CEO
Owners.com
America's largest FSBO marketplace

1 Why Sell FSBO?

WHY SELL YOUR house as a For Sale by Owner (FSBO)?

After all, there are close to a million agents available in the United States (and many more if you're in Canada or England) who would be more than willing to handle the sale for you. And, according to the National Association of REALTORS® (NAR®), more than 80 percent of home sellers use agents to sell their properties. Surely they can't all be wrong, can they?

Then there's timing. As real estate cycles between boom and bust, if we're on the downside, doesn't it just make more sense to use an agent? After all, aren't agents more likely to find you a buyer in a slower market than you are by yourself?

Sound right? I don't think so.

I've found there are some very compelling reasons to sell your home on your own. Here are three:

1. **You know your home best.** No one knows your home like you do. Not the appraiser, not the tax collector, and not the agent. You know why you bought it. You know its best features. And you're the person most likely to present it at its best and, thus, get the highest price.

   A few years ago, a study done in California compared the prices real estate agents got when they sold they own properties versus when they sold clients' homes. The result? The agents tended to get more for their own homes. The rationale was that they knew their own homes better and so were able to make a better presentation. This was reinforced more recently by a study that concluded that selling by owner, though taking longer, was more likely to fetch a higher price than selling through an agent.

You certainly want to get the most for your home, don't you?

2. **You can save a lot of money on the commission.** Few sellers will argue that the commission takes a big bite, often 6 percent of the sales price of the property. If the average home sells for around $200,000, over $12,000 of that will go toward commission. Wouldn't you rather keep that $12,000 in your pocket than hand it over to an agent?

This brings up an interesting point. The commission on a home sale is based on the selling price. Yet most people in reality don't own the full value of their home; in fact, the bank (or other lender) owns most of it.

If the average home is worth $200,000, then the average homeowner's equity is only around $50,000. The other $150,000 is typically in the form of a mortgage to a lender. (Unlike most other commodities, from rare coins to corn, houses are mostly financed.) Thus, while technically the home is in the seller's name for the full value, as a practical matter, the lender has the lion's share of it.

Is it really fair to pay a 6 percent commission on the full selling price when your equity is far less? Consider this situation: say you sell a $220,000 home and have only $55,000 in equity—the commission comes out to about 25 percent of that equity! (Figure it out: 6 percent of $220,000 is $13,200, which is nearly 25 percent of $55,000.)

In our example, when you pay the commission, you're not handing over just 6 percent—you might actually hand over a quarter or more of your interest in your property. That puts the commission in a whole new light.

Over the years, agents have discussed making the real estate commission a percentage of equity, not of the sales price. But as of this writing, no such plan that I know of has gained traction anywhere in the country.

All of which is to say, wouldn't you rather leave that commission in your pocket?

3. **You may be able to sell faster.** Finally, sometimes FSBOs sell faster than listed properties. It has a lot to do with how you handle that money you save on the commission.

If you intend to pocket it all, chances are the property will take you longer to sell, although perhaps at a better price.

On the other hand, if you're willing to give some of those savings to a buyer in the form of a discount, you may be able to sell faster. Consider, let's say the houses all around you are selling for $200,000, slightly below the national average. When you list at $200,000 at 6 percent, your actual net (after the commission), is roughly $188,000 (a $12,000 commission).

But, now let's say that instead of listing at $200,000, you put your home up for sale by owner at $193,000. You give the buyer a $7,000 discount.

We all know that in difficult markets, buyers are extremely price-sensitive. As a consequence (all else being equal), which property do you think a buyer is more likely to purchase? The listed house next door for $200,000? Or yours priced at $193,000? That should be a no-brainer.

And remember, when you sell for $193,000, that's your net. But the seller next-door, who's trying to sell for $200,000, will net only $188,000 after paying the commission. You net out $5,000 more. You not only may sell faster, but because you're not paying a commission, you'll make more money!

Quicker for more—that's hard to beat.

How Hard Is It?

Most people worry that it's hard to sell a home on their own. Yet it can't be that hard. Estimates are that something like 750,000 properties are sold by owner each year. If that many people can do it, how hard can it be?

Of course, there is some work involved. Most people who sell their own property don't expect it to be a free ride. They understand that they will need to do much of the work that an agent otherwise would do. But to save the commission, they are willing to do it.

What actually stops most people from selling their homes on their own are the three *F*s:

1. Lack of *f*acts
2. Lack of *f*orms
3. Presence of *f*ear

Lack of Facts

The old saying goes, "What you don't know *can* hurt you." But what you don't know also can be learned. Already, just reading this short distance into this book, you should know that it is possible to sell your own home—the fact that over the years, millions have successfully done so proves it.

As you go through the following pages, you'll learn many more facts about how to sell your home on your own. You'll learn how to prepare it to show (fix it up and "stage" it), you'll see how to negotiate with potential buyers, and you'll even walk through the transaction process to see how it's done.

Further, today the Internet provides hundreds of websites that cater to the by-owner seller. They provide FAQs, educational forums, question-and-answer sessions, videos, and much more. One of their goals is to get the information out to you so that you can sell your home on your own.

Read on and check the Internet (I'll suggest appropriate sites shortly), and you'll quickly build your knowledge. Today, not having the facts is an objection easily overcome.

Lack of Forms

Paperwork is another big stumbling block for most people. A great many sellers are enthusiastic about selling by owner but come to a complete halt when they don't have a piece of paper in their hands. How can they possibly sell their home without the right forms?

Relax. It's a different world out there today.

No, you don't need to rush down to the stationery store to look for real estate forms. Today's forms are largely standardized and available on the Internet (again, I'll list some of the websites shortly.) The cost is nominal, and you can download them quickly in the privacy of your own home.

What's more important, you need not (and should not) fill out the forms yourself. You can go online and hire a professional (attorney and/or agent) to help you fill out the forms for a flat fee. They can even modify them to suit your particular locale and deal.

In short, forms should no longer be a stumbling block.

Presence of Fear

Finally, the biggest stumbling block of all for most people who really want to sell their home on their own is fear. Fear can turn even the simplest project into something overwhelming.

Yet, as Franklin Delano Roosevelt said when speaking of the Great Depression, "The only thing we need fear, is fear itself." What do you have to fear about selling your own home? (Do you fear selling your own car?)

After all, if you own a home, you probably bought it (unless someone gave it to you). How difficult was your purchase transaction? Chances are an agent handled it. Couldn't you do what that agent did?

Remember, the vast majority of agents are ordinary people like you and me who simply chose the profession of selling real estate. Buy and sell a few houses and you, too, may decide to become an agent! (Agents have to pass a test and normally serve an apprenticeship.)

Most fears are irrational. We overcome them mainly through trial and error, through experience, through doing it. Sell one house on your own, and I assure you, you'll have virtually no fear about tackling the sale of the next one. Try it. Get started. And your fears will evaporate.

Where Do I Get Help?

Ten or 15 years ago, if you wanted to sell your home on your own, you really were on your own. Today, with the development of the Internet and sites that cater to by-owners/sellers, help is readily available.

To find a website that can provide you with forms, facts, and education, just type the key word *FSBO* in your Web browser. You'll find hundreds of sites ready to assist you.

Here are some of the more popular:

- *www.owners.com* (my personal favorite)
- *www.forsalebyowner.com*
- *www.fsbo.com*
- *www.homesbyowner.com*
- *www.virtualfsbo.com*

What About Preparing My Home for Sale?

What about it?

To sell your home quickly and for the best price, you need to get it prepared. It doesn't matter whether you're listing it or selling it by owner. The preparation should be the same.

If anything's broken, from a leaky roof to a cracked foundation, from a dripping faucet to an inoperative heater/air conditioner, you're going to have to fix it. In today's market, buyers expect every home to be in tiptop condition. If something isn't working, why should they buy your home when literally thousands of others have everything fixed? Any agent worth his salt will tell you this.

Further, to show it off at its best, you need to "stage" your home. Some agents will help you with the basics of this. Or, whether listing the home or selling by owner, you can hire a professional stager. Or you can check into chapter 7 in this book on staging and do it yourself. It's not hard once you understand the guidelines.

Fix it up, stage it, and you're ready to show it.

What About Marketing?

Agents market homes (or they're supposed to). When selling by owner, you're the one in charge of marketing. That's not hard to do, but it can take many forms:

- Put a sign out front (available from many by-owner websites).
- Send out flyers announcing the sale to everyone you know.
- Put *small* advertisements in the local paper.
- List with an online website (such as those noted above).
- List on the multiple-listing service (MLS) with a "flat-fee MLS" listing. *Flat-fee* refers to a nominal fee of around $400 for simply listing your

property on the MLS that some agents associated with FSBO websites charge; it does not include the services of an agent to help with the sale of the home. (See below for a detailed explanation.)

The MLS is a hugely successful tool that agents use to cooperate on listings. When you list with an agent, your home normally goes up on the MLS. From there, other agents in your area can see that your home is available and can bring by their buyers, thus facilitating a sale.

Further, homes listed on the MLS are normally also listed online at *www.realtor.com*. This is probably the most viewed real estate site in the country. Many listings are also picked up by other very popular sites such as *www.aol.com* and *www.yahoo.com*.

What's important to understand here is that somewhere between 75 and 80 percent of *all* potential home buyers *first* check out listings on the Internet. Thus, getting your house exposed on the MLS and popular real estate Internet sites is a great way to get exposure; in other words, you do it the same way agents do it.

KEY CONCEPT   *As a bonus, listing on the MLS exposes you not only to agents but also to buyers, some of whom are checking the listings but are not working with agents. Thus, assuming you've done a flat fee MLS listing with the agent, it might lead to a FSBO sale. (Unfortunately, MLS listings frequently only carry the agent's phone number, but they typically do carry the property address.)*

But how do you get on the MLS if you don't list with an agent? (As of this writing, only homes listed by REALTOR® agents can go up on the MLS.)

The answer is the flat-fee MLS listing noted above. For a fee that's usually around $400, an agent can list your home on the MLS. As a consequence, you should get exposure on the many related websites. (The agent usually won't provide any services for you, except for the listing, so you're still selling by owner.)

Now your home can be on the heavily visited websites, and when potential buyers are looking for listings, your home will be right there with the rest (including written description, price, and photo). Online websites such as *www.*

owners.com provide a service for flat-fee listings, having a broker in your area contact you to handle the job. (We'll say more about this in chapter 4.)

All of which is to say that the Internet tools for marketing your property are powerful and readily available. Today, marketing your property on your own is a level playing field—you can successfully compete with agents.

What About Selling in a Tough Market?

This question brings us full circle and touches on many of the areas we've discussed, including fear, facts, and marketing. The question is really, "Can I sell my home by owner in a down market, or can I only do it when the market's booming (or going sideways)?"

The answer is that the number of people selling by owner is pretty much the same regardless of what the market is doing. Whether it's going up, down, or sideways doesn't seem to make much of a difference.

I suppose that when the market's up, there's a perception that it's easier to sell because homes are moving faster in general. But buyers often prefer to use agents in this market to help them be the first to make an offer and to keep a lid on price.

When the market's down or going sideways, the perception is that it can be harder for an owner to find a buyer because there are fewer buyers out there. But that theory doesn't take into account the level playing field with regard to marketing.

Further, when by-owner sellers give discounts, they often move their homes faster.

 KEY CONCEPT   *Don't worry about the market. Look at where you can get the most money for your home . . . and move it the quickest.*

My best suggestion is that if you're at all considering selling by owner, you give it a try. Take a set amount of time—a month, six weeks, three months, or whatever—and try selling by owner. Remember, if things don't work out, you can always fall back on listing with a real estate agent as your plan B.

2 Test Yourself: Are You Suited to Selling FSBO?

MANY OF US believe that salespeople are born, not made. There are those, we think, who can easily sell ice cubes to Inuits and sunlamps to Tahitians.

Perhaps you're that sort of individual? If so, you should be able to sell your house on your own by next weekend without my or anybody else's help.

On the other hand, if you're a normal human being, you may get along fairly well with people, but you don't have any super talents when it comes to selling. Rest assured, you don't need any.

I have found that when selling real estate, or anything else for that matter, there are two keys to success: (1) knowing what you are selling and (2) gaining the trust of the buyer.

If you really know your product, chances are you can sell it. (That's why great salespeople spend a lot of their time learning every detail about what they are selling.) And there you have the big advantage when selling your own home. After all, who knows it better than you?

The other requirement is establishing trust. For most of us, this comes naturally— it's mainly just being straightforward and honest. It's just establishing rapport with a would-be buyer. There are even rules for doing it that we'll go into at the end of this chapter.

Sound simple? It really is.

Nevertheless, many people who would be quite successful at selling FSBO shy away from it, fearing that they don't have the wherewithal to actually pull off a sale. They worry that they won't be able to find a buyer. Or that, if they do find a buyer, they won't be able to convince her to make the purchase. Or that, if they do get a buyer ready, willing, and able to make the purchase, they won't know how to conclude the sale. Perhaps you're one of these worriers?

If so, here's a little quiz. It will help you make up your mind about whether or not you should sell by owner.

Keep in mind that there are no right or wrong answers and you can't fail the test. The entire goal is to get a handle on your FSBO potential. Who knows: you may discover that you are a natural-born by-owner seller!

Test—Are You Suited to Selling by Owner?

Answer each of the following questions *YES* or *NO*.

Motivation

1. Do you want to save money on the sale of your home? Yes ☐ No ☐
2. Do you want to sell for more? Yes ☐ No ☐
3. Do you want a quicker sale? Yes ☐ No ☐
4. Do you want to control all aspects of the sale? Yes ☐ No ☐
5. Do you want to learn the intricacies of a real estate transaction? Yes ☐ No ☐
6. Do you want to learn more about investing in real estate? Yes ☐ No ☐
7. Do you want to do it yourself? Yes ☐ No ☐

Knowledge

1. Do you know when your home was built? Yes ☐ No ☐
2. Do you know its best points? Yes ☐ No ☐
3. Do you know its worst points? Yes ☐ No ☐
4. Do you know why the location is good/bad? Yes ☐ No ☐
5. Do you know the local schools? Yes ☐ No ☐
6. Do you know the local crime rates? Yes ☐ No ☐

Salesmanship

1. Can you greet strangers and welcome them into your home?   Yes ☐ No ☐
2. Do you mind showing people every nook and cranny of your house?   Yes ☐ No ☐
3. Can you avoid being argumentative?   Yes ☐ No ☐
4. Are you willing to be completely honest about your home?   Yes ☐ No ☐
5. Are you willing to make the buyer respect you by never lying, hiding, or promising what you can't deliver?   Yes ☐ No ☐
6. Are you willing to negotiate over price and terms?   Yes ☐ No ☐
7. Can you encourage and coach a buyer who might be unfamiliar with closing a real estate transaction?   Yes ☐ No ☐

Marketing

1. Are you willing to put a For Sale sign up in your front yard?   Yes ☐ No ☐
2. Will you create flyers describing your home (with a photo)?   Yes ☐ No ☐
3. Will you answer phone calls and respond to potential buyers?   Yes ☐ No ☐
4. Will you spread the word about your sale to everyone you know?   Yes ☐ No ☐
5. Will you list with an online by-owner website?   Yes ☐ No ☐
6. Will you pay for a flat-fee MLS listing?   Yes ☐ No ☐
7. Will you cooperate with brokers who may want to help you sell (see chapter 10)?   Yes ☐ No ☐

Fixing Up

1. Will you fix any damage to your home *before* putting it up for sale?   Yes ☐ No ☐
2. Will you paint the front, the entry, and any other area that looks shabby?   Yes ☐ No ☐
3. Will you repair the driveway?   Yes ☐ No ☐
4. Will you trim the hedges, grow the lawn green, and add colorful flowers to the front?   Yes ☐ No ☐
5. Will you replace or at least clean the carpets?   Yes ☐ No ☐
6. Will you make the kitchen and bathrooms spotless?   Yes ☐ No ☐
7. Will you repair any broken systems (heating, cooling, water, drainage, and so on)?   Yes ☐ No ☐

Staging

1. Will you get rid of the clutter?   Yes ☐ No ☐
2. Will you remove all of your personal items (such as family photos)?   Yes ☐ No ☐
3. Will you deodorize (especially if you have pets)?   Yes ☐ No ☐
4. Will you add light fixtures to brighten your home?   Yes ☐ No ☐
5. Will you add flowers to colorize your rooms?   Yes ☐ No ☐
6. Are you willing to rearrange your furniture or even rent new furniture to show off your home?   Yes ☐ No ☐
7. Will you consult with a professional stager, or at least an agent, about what else needs to be done to show your home at its best?   Yes ☐ No ☐

Paperwork

1. Are you willing to read books such as this and go to by-owner websites online to learn what paperwork is involved in a sale?   Yes ☐ No ☐
2. Are you willing to download documents?   Yes ☐ No ☐
3. Will you contact professionals (such as an attorney or an agent) who are available online?   Yes ☐ No ☐
4. Will you pay a professional a flat fee to draw up legal documents for you?   Yes ☐ No ☐
5. Will you help educate your buyer as to the documentation necessary?   Yes ☐ No ☐
6. Will you fill out disclosure forms to present to a buyer?   Yes ☐ No ☐
7. Will you handle any other paperwork that may crop up?   Yes ☐ No ☐

Closing

1. Will you open an escrow account (either locally or online)?   Yes ☐ No ☐
2. Will you track the buyer's attempts to get financing?   Yes ☐ No ☐
3. Will you sign the deed and provide any documentation necessary to close?   Yes ☐ No ☐
4. Will you pay your share of title and escrow charges?   Yes ☐ No ☐
5. Will you get a termite clearance, if needed, and any other clearance the buyer's lender may require?   Yes ☐ No ☐
6. Will you clear the title of any problems it may have as explained by the escrow officer?   Yes ☐ No ☐
7. Will you conduct a final walkthrough with the buyer?   Yes ☐ No ☐

As you go through these questions, what should immediately strike you (if you've ever bought or sold a home) is that they're the same steps that everyone has to go through to sell any home. Most of them you'll need to do *whether or not* you use an agent. It's just that if you sell FSBO, you'll need to do all of them yourself. Are you ready for that?

To find out, add up all your yes answers. Here's how to score:

40–49: YES. Why are you hesitating? You're a natural-born FSBO seller. Time to get started!

30–39: YES. You should do well selling by owner. But you still lack confidence. Work at getting all the knowledge you can about real estate sales. In addition to reading this book, check into online educational forums.

20–39: YES? You're on the fence. You probably would like to save the commission, but you're hesitant about making the commitment to sell by owner. Spend some time thinking about that commission you're getting ready to give an agent.

10–19: YES? I suspect you're the sort who would simply like to pay someone else to do it for you. You probably would hire a plumber before fixing a washer or hire an accountant instead of doing your own taxes. Yet selling your home on your own can be an adventure, something new and different, that could add spice to your life (in addition to saving you money). You'll do well if you view it as a challenge.

0–9: YES! Hire an agent.

More About Trust

As I mentioned at the beginning of this chapter, establishing trust is vital when selling any product, including your home. No buyer will be willing to purchase directly from you unless and until he first trusts you.

Yet we sometimes do things that can diminish trust. These may seem innocent at first, but over time, they poison the water and make it impossible to conclude a deal. Things I'm talking about include these:

- Forget to mention those bad things about your house that the buyer soon discovers on her own.

- Exaggerate the good points of your home (for example, "This neighborhood is *always* quiet," "This house is huge—you'll *never* need a bigger one," or, "There's no way you'll *ever* need to wash the carpet—it *always* stays clean.") Absolute words like *always, never,* and *ever* can do you in.
- Promise the buyer the world, hoping he won't remember what you said.
- And so on...

Always remember that as the seller of a home dealing directly with a buyer, you are suspect. The buyer suspects that you might do anything and everything to sell that home, including lying and cheating. The buyer sees you as an adversary.

Therefore, if you're going to deal effectively with that buyer and come to acceptable terms in a successful sale, you have to prove your trustworthiness.

How to Prove to a Buyer That You're Trustworthy
Stand Your Ground

Basically, this comes down to meaning what you say and saying what you mean. However, it's far easier to say than to do.

If, for example, you're proud of your rosebushes but the buyer says that your favorite looks like a weed, you don't have to agree. To do that would be toadying. And the buyer would realize you were kowtowing and immediately distrust whatever else you had to say.

Of course, you don't have to get into an argument, either. You can simply point out that roses come in all shapes and sizes. Some people like them, while others don't.

If the buyer says that the color you've painted the stones over your fireplace is hideous, you don't have to get defensive, but neither do you have to agree that, yes, you could have done better than florid pink over river stones. Instead, you can simply nod, acknowledging the buyer's opinion, and move on.

The point is simple. If buyers begin to suspect that'll you'll agree with whatever they say, how can they trust you to tell them the truth? On the other hand, if you don't change your opinion to suit them, they'll come to respect you and, over time, trust what you say...which is critical to making a deal.

Don't Hide Defects

We all know that a defect in the house, from a simple wall crack to a leaky roof, will bring down the price and might even lead a buyer to forgo making an offer. Therefore, the temptation is to hide the defect—paint over the crack or the discolored ceiling.

However, almost always if you attempt to hide a defect, it will come out sooner or later. And as soon as the buyer discovers that you've been hiding something, she will distrust you. As a result, a buyer who might otherwise be willing to go ahead with the sale, accepting a defect or negotiating to have it fixed, will now wonder what else you've concealed. And the deal may be lost. Remember, a buyer who distrusts you won't want to deal with you.

Never Lie

You state that the roof is perfect; it never leaks. But the buyer discovers water stains in the attic. You attempt to cover your tracks by saying it's just from a leaking pipe that was fixed.

Then the buyer notices pinpoints of light coming through the shingles. What can she conclude except that you're a liar? Without trust, a potential deal could be lost.

Never Promise Something You Can't Do

You say that you know all about real estate financing and you'll help the buyer get a loan. You promise that the buyer can qualify for a 90 percent loan, but after he agrees to buy, you both discover that the maximum loan the buyer can get is 80 percent. The buyer can't complete the purchase as negotiated and, feeling cheated, won't come up with more money. The deal is lost.

KEY CONCEPT *If you conceal, lie, or even exaggerate, little inconsistencies will do you in every time. Buyers, who are naturally suspicious, are looking for those inconsistencies. Honesty is the key to establishing rapport with the buyer. The buyer doesn't have to like you (although that does help), but the buyer must trust you if the two of you are to conclude a successful real estate sale.*

Getting to Trust

In short, always work at establishing trust by

- Standing your ground;
- Not hiding defects;
- Never lying; and
- Never promising something you can't deliver.

If you abide by these rules, the buyer will soon see that you are someone with whom he can work—someone he can count on. The buyer will want to deal with you. If you don't establish trust, you'll find that distrust sours every potential buyer who walks in the door.

The Bottom Line

I can't predict whether you'll be a great FSBO seller or a terrible one. In fact, you'll never know until you try.

That's why I suggest that at the least, you give it a trial period. Set a time frame, whether it's a week, a month, or three months. Read through this book to see what's involved and then attempt it. Who knows, you may get lucky and sell your home on your own the first week out!

You'll never know unless you try.

3 Seven Key Steps to Finding a Buyer and Selling

FOR MOST PEOPLE, there's a sense of mystery about selling a home. They feel agents can do it because they have the arcane wisdom. Many sellers, however, fear they themselves can't do it because they don't have the key to unlock the mystery.

In truth, however, selling your home is as open and easy as anything else you set your mind to, from driving a car to playing golf or tennis.

Of course, some of us do it better than others. But that's usually because we know the key steps involved in the process. Want to improve your golf game? Take some lessons. Want to sell your house tomorrow? Read up on the process of finding a buyer and conducting a sale!

Here are the seven key steps you need to follow to find a buyer quickly and sell your home by owner. You'll find these aren't hard. And all the tools you need are readily accessible.

Key Step 1: Assess the Market and Come Up with a Price

When the real estate market is booming, you can ask almost any ridiculous price, and chances are you'll get it. When the market turns soft, however, it's a different world. Today, if you want to hook a buyer and pull off a sale, you need to price your home realistically. That may mean offering it for less than you hoped it would be worth.

KEY CONCEPT *Your home is worth only what a buyer is willing to pay for it. It doesn't matter what you have put into it, how much you originally paid, or what it was worth last year. The only thing that counts is the present— what's it worth to a buyer today?*

Do You Know What Your Home Is Worth?

Most sellers believe they do. After all, most sellers follow the prices in their neighborhood. Whenever a nearby home sells, they check it out, meaning they find out the sales price and then figure their home is probably worth a little bit more.

But do you really know the value of your home? In truth, very few sellers do.

The reality is that most sellers are emotionally involved with their property. They know how much they paid for it and know the costs of what they've put into it. They dearly remember the blood, sweat, and perhaps even tears those improvements cost. And, understandably, they want every penny back, plus a profit.

Unfortunately, the truth is that what sellers want for a home has nothing at all to do with what it's worth. It's worth only what the market will bear. And who knows the market best? The buyers!

Surprisingly to most sellers, most buyers, after only a few days of house hunting, know the market pretty well. After all, they've looked at a lot of available homes. They've been comparing locations, sizes, and features. After a dozen or so homes, they begin to get a pretty good handle on value.

On the other hand, chances are as a seller, you haven't seen all the other homes for sale. You haven't compared locations, sizes, and features. As a result, you are not up on the market.

You may think your house is worth what the highest-priced house on your street sold for two years ago. You may feel it's worth the sum total of what you've spent on plants, weed control, carpeting, upgrading, and painting. You may feel it's worth what the mortgage appraiser or the county tax assessor valued it at.

The most chilling phrase I know of when appraising real estate is when a seller says, "I have a price in mind." The truth is that it doesn't matter what price you have in mind. Your house is worth what the market says it's worth (and what savvy buyers are willing to pay)—not a dime more.

Tough words. But pay heed to them. Nothing keeps a house from selling more than overpricing it.

FSBOs Don't Sell for More

In today's market, price is critical. It is almost as critical as location. Houses that are priced right will, in fact, sell. Those that are priced too high will sit there. However, the biggest mistake you can make is to think, "Because I'm selling FSBO, I can ask more money for my house."

Of course, you probably won't make this critical error, but if you know of others who are selling FSBO, remind them that buyers see things differently than sellers. Buyers don't care if the house is listed, FSBO, or auctioned. They are interested in only one thing after location, and that's price. Give the buyers the right price, and they'll buy.

To you, selling FSBO probably is a significant undertaking. It may mean that you're putting in lots of time and effort. And you may be spending big bucks fixing up the house. It's only natural, therefore, that as a FSBO seller, you want to recoup your time, money, and effort from the buyer. It's not unreasonable to feel that you are entitled to ask more for your house.

To repeat: The unfortunate truth is that, entitled or not, you can get only what the house is worth on the market. You can ask anything that you want, but you will only get what buyers are willing to pay.

As I said, price it too high, and your house will sit there, languishing, while other homes, priced only a few thousand less, may sell in days.

How Do I Determine the Right Price?

I hope I've convinced you to price your home right. But what is the right price?

The first step here is to get a comparative market analysis (CMA). Here, you get a list of all of the homes similar to yours that have sold in your area over the past 6 to 12 months. (These properties are called *comps*.) Then you compare them by location, sizes, and features, adding to the value of your house if it is better in some way (such as a choicer location) and subtracting if it lacks a feature (such as a swimming pool).

Where do you get a CMA? Almost any real estate agent will be willing to provide one for you in the hopes that you'll eventually list with him. (Check out chapter 10 on finding an agent to work with you.) You can also do the work entirely yourself by using the Internet. The site *www.zillow.com* provides recent home sales price for free. Many other websites offer to create a CMA for a nominal fee; try *www.realestateyahoo.com* and *www.realestateabc.com*.

But if you do your own CMA, be careful. You have to be scrupulously honest. Remember, you can't tilt the scales in your favor. Buyers are doing CMAs all the time on their own as they tour homes, and they know value. Price your home just a little too high, and they'll discard it as an option.

Adjust for Market Conditions

When prices are going up, I always suggest adding a few percent to the price you're asking to compensate for market increases since your comps sold. Why leave anything on the table when buyers will pay more?

When the market is going down, you have to do the opposite. You need to take a few percentage points off the price to get to where the market is since the comps sold.

Recently I was involved in the sale of a home in Sacramento, California. This market was red hot up until about 2006, with prices jumping as much as 25 percent a year.

Since then, however, it has turned cold, with prices falling precipitously. The inventory in the area soared. There were thousands of homes for sale, and there were few buyers, with most scared off because of the declining prices.

But we (it was my son's home) wanted to sell. So I advised dropping the price 5 to 10 percent below the CMA.

My son was shocked. Why take such a big hit, he wondered. Why not simply sell for market price?

 KEY CONCEPT *In a down market, you have to get ahead of the curve. To sell, you need to offer a bargain, a price below current market. It's the only way to entice fearful buyers.*

Because, I explained, to entice a buyer in a falling market, you need to show that you're selling where the market will be tomorrow, not necessarily where it is today. If buyers perceive they are getting a bargain (a price below market), it helps allay their fear of a falling market. By paying your price, they'll get ahead of the market and have a cushion should it fall further.

My son agreed. In a terrible market with lots of sellers, few buyers, and almost no sales, he sold within two weeks.

At first he was a bit sorry he had sold for so little. After all, the same model home had sold for tens of thousands of dollars more only five or six months earlier.

The proof, however, is in the results. Within a few months, many of the homes like his were sitting on the market, unsold, with an asking price tens of thousands of dollars less than he'd sold for. By quickly dropping his price and getting ahead of the curve, he had gotten out with, as it turned out, a great price.

Pricing right is key to selling in a tight market. (See chapter 8 for more information on pricing.)

Key Step 2: Dress Your Home for Sale

Think of your home as a chocolate cake. You can present this cake in two ways. One way is just as the ingredients. Place flour, water, cocoa, eggs, yeast, sugar, and food coloring in front of most people, and they'll look at it dispassionately and say, "Ho hum." However, mix up all the ingredients, bake it, and then present them with the finished product. Their eyes will go wide, and they'll say, "Yum, a chocolate cake!"

Home buyers are no different. Present them with a yard filled with weeds, a front that's got peeling paint, soiled carpeting, scratches on the walls, clutter in the rooms, poor lighting, and so on, and they're going to say, "Ho hum."

On the other hand, say you fix the place up. Trim the hedges and replant the front lawn. Repaint the front of the home and some of the interior. Put in new carpeting or at the least clean the old carpeting. Remove the clutter. Depersonalize and get rid of any odors.

Now you've dressed your home for sale. Buyers who come by will immediately see it at its best. They'll begin thinking to themselves, "This is a house I could live in!"

K E Y   C O N C E P T *Don't underestimate curb appeal, potential buyers' first impression of your home. It often makes or breaks a sale.*

Make the effort. Do the work. It won't cost that much, take that much time, or be that hard to do. Getting your property ready for buyers is essential if you want to sell, especially in a down market. For more clues on exactly what to do and how much to spend, check out chapters 6 and 7.

Key Step 3: Prepare a Marketing Campaign

Don't keep the fact that you're selling FSBO a secret. Tell everyone you know.

Get your own sign and display it prominently in your front yard. (Many online FSBO services will offer a sign to you for a nominal charge.) Prepare leaflets describing your property, including a picture, and distribute them widely. Build an information box and attach it to your sign. Put flyers up on bulletin boards in public buildings, the housing offices of corporations, and even on display panels in supermarkets.

And advertise. Your ad doesn't have to be big, but it should run regularly. Also, you should change it often so that buyers don't recognize your house as the same property and ignore it.

Also, find out whether inexpensive advertising is available on local radio and cable TV stations. (It often is.) Try a 30-second commercial. The right slant can bring you amazing results. (We'll have more to say on advertising in chapter 9.)

Talk up your property to all of your acquaintances, whether or not they're interested in buying. Someone may know a friend of a friend who's interested, and that person might ultimately become your buyer.

Finally, list with an online FSBO service, such as *www.owners.com* or *www. fsbo.com.* They can provide education, encouragement, and, perhaps most important, a way to list your home for a flat fee on the MLS. (See chapter 4 for more on online help.)

Agents use the MLS to work together. There might be as many as a thousand or more agents in your area. If a home is listed on the MLS, it's available to all of them. Also, when you list on the MLS, your listing is normally picked up and placed on *www.realtor.com* and other popular online services. Remember, currently over 80 percent of home buyers first check the Internet when looking for a home. When you list on the MLS, you increase your exposure a thousand times over, both to buyers who are working with agents and buyers who are working on their own.

By the way, here's a tip you may not have considered: be friendly with real estate agents when they come by (and they will!). Tell them that right now you're trying to sell on your own as a FSBO, but if you don't sell within a reasonable time, you'll consider working through them. Tell them also that you'll pay a buyer's agent commission (typically half the usual rate) if they find a buyer.

Remember, real estate agents are in the business of finding buyers. It would be foolish to ignore them, particularly when you can get them to work for you. (See chapter 10 for details on how to get agents to work for you.)

Key Step 4: Show Your Home

Making the commitment to sell FSBO means having your home clean, tidy, and ready to show at a moment's notice. Unfortunately, it also means giving up some of your free time. You must be willing to wait for buyers to show up. If a buyer calls you at 8:00 AM Sunday while you're still sleeping, you'll agree to show the property at 9:00 AM, even though it means jumping out of bed and working frantically to get the place ready.

Being available for buyers means keeping at least one phone line clear. If you're going to be gone, it means using call forwarding, an answering machine, a cell phone, or a family member to catch incoming calls. It means that you're ready to show the house every day of the week and that it's clean all of those days.

Don't bother to sell FSBO unless you're willing to do all of the tasks described. If you're half-hearted about it, if you decide to take a two-week vacation three days after putting the sign in the front yard, if you tell a buyer who calls that you've got to go to your mother's house for lunch and can't show the property, then don't bother to sell FSBO. List with an agent instead.

When you list with yourself, you must make the commitments necessary to sell your home successfully. One of the biggest commitments is time. If you can't spend the time, list with an agent who can. A FSBO seller must show the house. That's just the way it is.

Until you get their signatures on the dotted line, you're a slave to potential buyers. To think anything else is to do yourself a disservice. To attempt to sell FSBO without making yourself and the property always available is simply playing games.

If you truly want to sell FSBO, you'll make the time. If you find that you simply can't, then I urge you to reconsider listing with a full-service agent.

Key Step 5: Sell and Negotiate

If the truth be known, selling your home starts the moment the potential buyer walks into your home and you shake hands. (Always greet potential buyers in a friendly matter, get their names including their first names, and shake hands. It helps set up rapport.)

 K E Y   C O N C E P T *Most buyers are looking for reasons to reject the property. Your goal is to give them reasons to want it.*

Assuming your home shines (see Key Step 2), other issues will arise. There's the overall layout of the house and yard, as well as location-related matters such as schools, hospitals, crime rates, shopping access, and so on.

While you should definitely give potential buyers time to stroll through your home and get a feel for it, you should also plan time to answer their questions.

Most buyers, for example, will ask about the schools in the area (unless they are already familiar with them). You goal is to reassure them of the fine quality of your schools or at least that they are getting better. Remember, the better the schools, the more likely you are to get an offer—and a better offer.

What you're really looking for are the buyers to begin saying that they *don't like* this or that. Usually only when the buyer begins telling you negatives do negotiations begin in earnest.

When the buyers compliment everything and tell you what a wonderful home you have, they're probably not interested. They're just humoring you until they can leave and get on with their search.

When they begin to find fault, then they are looking at the house as if it were their own. They're trying to see how their furniture would fit, how much repair and repainting they would have to do, whether the home is too big or too small, and most importantly, how much their negatives might influence you to drop your price.

Always be pleasant and cordial. And try to turn a negative into a positive. For example, the buyers complain the backyard is too small, so you point out how little maintenance it requires. When you can't turn around a negative, simply acknowledge it and move on.

Eventually, the buyers will begin to sound really interested. When that happens, suggest that they may want to discuss price and terms with you. If they do, feel free to tell them what you want out of the property, but always leave the door open to them by saying that, of course, "everything is negotiable."

With some buyers, agreement will come quickly, and you're off to the purchase agreement (see below). Others will want to come back half a dozen times before they're ready to deal. And they may come back with their own negotiator—an agent, a friend, a relative, an attorney, or whomever. Be prepared to negotiate calmly.

 K E Y   C O N C E P T *The key to getting what you want in negotiations is to know what you want. Know your own bottom line.*

Key Step 6: Sign Up the Buyer and Handle the Paperwork

When you've got your buyer ready to sign on the dotted line, be sure you have a dotted line for her to sign on. In chapter 13, we'll talk about how to work with the buyer to prepare a sales agreement. You'll definitely want either an agent and/or an attorney to prepare such an agreement for you.

On the other hand, if you're cobrokering with an agent (for half a commission) and the agent brings in the buyer, he should handle the preparation of the purchase agreement. Just remember: the agent is most likely not on your side—he's on the buyer's side. So know what you're doing or pay a flat fee to get professional flat fee help on your side. (See chapter 4.)

The sales agreement is the most important document of the sale as it governs all the others. Once you have a completely filled out and signed sales agreement, you'll need to open an escrow account (unless the buyer's agent is also handling this for you).

Of course, there's other paperwork involved. You'll need to give the buyer disclosures. These forms can be obtained from an agent or from an online FSBO site, and a sample is provided at the end of this book. (See also chapter 13 for more information on handling the paperwork.)

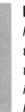

K E Y   C O N C E P T *Before you sign any deal, be sure that the buyer has the means to buy. This usually takes the form of a solid pre-approval letter showing she has been approved by a lender for enough money to make the purchase. It also means the buyer puts up a deposit to show she is earnest in making the purchase. And you may want to confirm with a bank (with the buyer's permission) that she has enough cash on hand for the down payment.*

Key Step 7: Close the Deal

Once you've got the buyer signed up, there remains a period during which all of the loose ends of the deal are put together. You (or the buyer or his agent, if one is involved) will open escrow with an escrow company. This is a third party who handles the paperwork, the money, and the title.

There are lots of escrow companies, many of them found online, and you should shop around for the one that offers you the lowest prices. You may need to pay for escrow services and possibly title insurance for the buyer.

Usually, an escrow account runs for 30 to 45 days. How long is determined by need and what's written into the sales agreement. Who pays what for escrow is determined by local custom. The escrow officer can clue you into the usual arrangements in your area. (See also chapter 16 for details on handling the closing.)

Chances are, your buyers will want a home inspection, and you'll need to provide them with disclosures. Look into chapter 12 for details on this. The important thing here is that you comply with deadlines and disclose all defects. You don't want a buyer coming back years later to hound you over a problem that turns up because of something that you failed to disclose.

Also, should there be a defect in your title, you'll need to clear it up. A defect is something such as a lien you forgot to pay off years ago. Perhaps you were sued by a credit company and they filed against the property. Or perhaps there was a court settlement that was paid off, but the records never reflected it. It's up to you to solve the problem. (Check with an attorney on these issues. Also see chapter 16 on closing.)

 KEY CONCEPT *During escrow, periodically you'll want to check in with the buyers to make sure that they are progressing with their mortgage. Remember, if for any reason they can't get a mortgage, chances are you will lose your deal.*

If all goes well (and usually it does), there will come a day when you are notified that escrow is ready to close. Just before it does, however, the buyers may want a "final walkthrough," which allows them to see that the house is just as it was when they originally made the offer. (See chapter 16 for details on this.)

For you, as the seller, there's not much more to do after this than to approve the final escrow instructions, which say who gets paid for what, and sign off on the deed to be given to the buyer.

Just remember, however, that Rome wasn't built in a day. Most seemingly instant successes are the result of repeated attempts after repeated failures. Most of those who succeed aren't any brighter, more industrious, or more knowledgeable than you. Closing the deal typically takes 30 to 45 days, sometimes longer. And during that time, all sorts of problems can occur. Things can go wrong!

Just go with the flow. Maintain a positive attitude, and most problems will be solved.

Finally, when the buyer and the lender deposit funds, the escrow will close, and you'll get a call saying your check is ready to be picked up. Chances are it will be one of the best days of your life!

You, Too, Can Sell Your House FSBO

However, you may not be able to sell it the first day or the first week, or even the first month. Time may become a bit of an enemy.

You may get tired of staying home on weekends waiting for someone to call or knock on your door. Or, suddenly, three or four people will call and then come by, interrupting whatever you've planned. Or you'll spend so much time cleaning and polishing, painting and trimming, that you'll be sick of it. You'll begin to tell yourself you need a vacation from house selling!

In the short term, you may come to resent your house and the process of selling it.

That's okay as long as you don't give up. Hang in there. Your buyer will show up. And then one bright day, your house will be sold!

4 Get Expert Help Online

ONE OF THE first and biggest questions that sellers ask when considering selling FSBO is, "Where do I get the information and knowledge I need to conduct the sale?"

One answer, of course, is in this very book. Hopefully, it will provide you with not only the basics but advanced help as well.

Another answer is to go online. For specific questions you may have, nothing can beat the expert help that's offered online. In this chapter, we'll look at just what's available on the Internet and how to find it.

Not the Old Internet FSBO Sites

Selling by owner online got started over a decade ago, with hundreds of sites popping up telling you they could quickly and easily sell your home, if only you listed with them. Often the price was only a few hundred dollars, which when compared to the traditional agent's commission seemed ridiculously cheap. Many people opted for it.

However, the model for these early sites was basically flawed. They attempted to do over the Internet what the agent did in person. They attempted to provide full-service selling with the seller doing next to nothing.

Since selling FSBO requires the seller to participate and since only a physical real estate agent can provide true full service, most of these sites were doomed to failure. By the dot-com crash at the turn of the century, many were already out of business.

Those owners who did list on Internet sites were often sadly disappointed. There were few referrals and few buyers. The seller's listing dollars were, basically, wasted. The early FSBO sites were mostly a promise unfulfilled.

However, a few older sites remain, and new ones have emerged. Most of these have changed with the times, adopted new business models, and emerged as healthy partners offering just the kind of expert help that sellers who want to sell on their own need. *www.owners.com*. Wit

A site such as Owners.com, for example, supplies all sorts of educational support. Additionally, other companies and individuals associated with real estate selling support this site and others. These include the following:

- Lenders
- Title/escrow companies
- Home inspection companies
- Home warranty companies
- Attorneys
- Educational services (books, magazines, and so on featuring real estate)
- Agents who will accept flat fees for limited services, such as listing a property on the MLS
- And more

Many of today's sites operate according to a different concept from their predecessors. They fully understand that when you sell by owner, you're going to have to perform much of the work that the agent would otherwise perform. The sites don't claim to do it for you. Instead, they give you the tools you need to do it yourself.

For example, you'll need something as simple as a yard sign. Where do you get it?

Of course, you can go to your local hardware store and get a basic For Sale sign and stick in your front lawn. But it will look amateurish and may scare timid buyers away.

Or you can go to a professional sign painter to have a fancy sign made for you at the cost of several hundred dollars.

Or you can go to any number of FSBO websites and, for a nominal fee, have them send you a sign. Sometimes these signs will include your phone number and a Web address where information on your home can be found.

Ideally the sign you get will display an automated answering service telephone number. The service allows sellers to protect their privacy while making it easy for buyers to learn about their properties. Buyers can call the toll-free answering service number 24/7 to learn basic information (size, bedrooms, bathrooms, square feet) and leave messages for sellers. FSBO sellers really enjoy the privacy aspect, as it allows them to avoid unsolicited calls from agents.

Today's sites can provide the following information and features:

- Expertise
- Links to companies that offer forms
- Signs
- A place to show images of your property
- Pricing information
- Mortgage information
- Legal aid
- Information on disclosures
- Suggestions for professional inspections
- Links to escrow and title services
- Home warranty plans
- Insurance
- Phone message service
- MLS listing service (for a flat fee)
- Support
- And more

In effect, the Internet sites provide what you need to sell your home on your own.

A Level Playing Field

The effect of the new online sites is to level the playing field so you can compete successfully with agents. Before the agents had all the tools. Now you have access to them too.

Let's take an example to see how this works. Marc and Caroline decide to sell their home. They definitely are interested in saving the money (or at least part of it) that they would otherwise spend on an agent's commission. So they decide on a price, and for a nominal fee, they list the property on an Internet site like *www.owners.com*.

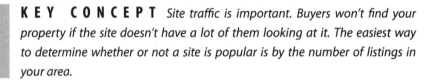

KEY CONCEPT *Site traffic is important. Buyers won't find your property if the site doesn't have a lot of them looking at it. The easiest way to determine whether or not a site is popular is by the number of listings in your area.*

The first thing that happens is that they get a sign to put in front of their home. Along with the sign comes a wealth of information on how to sell by owner.

Next they fill out a form that gives a complete description of their home along with some paragraphs that extol its features and should help sell it, all of which goes up on the site at a specific address that buyers can access.

Then they shoot some pictures of their home on their digital camera and send those to the site, which puts them up next to their home's description.

When Caroline and Marc put that sign in front of their home, they don't just put their phone number on it. They also list the home's Web address. (For privacy, they may not even put their phone number on the sign at all.)

When a prospective buyer drives by and sees their sign, she copies down the Web address and, instead of calling them directly, looks up the house at the Internet site. There the buyer can learn all the specifics from price to terms, from number of bedrooms and bathrooms to square feet, from amenities such as a pool or spa to local school districts.

Furthermore, Marc and Caroline compose an advertisement for the local paper, relying on educational information their website provides. The ad typically is short, only three or four lines. (You'll learn how to write these in chapter 9.)

Potential buyers who see the ad and want more information can go to the website to see pictures of the house and learn more about it. Further, because these sites typically provide related links, the buyers can get information on how big a loan they can get pre-approved for. In other words, they can find out quickly if they qualify to buy Marc and Caroline's home.

Caroline and Marc also distribute flyers promoting their home at their place of work, tack them up on bulletin boards in grocery stores, leave them at the housing offices of nearby corporations, and so on. By the way, Internet listings can make great marketing brochures.

In each of these cases, Caroline and Marc refer prospective buyers to their home's website address. People who see the flyer and want to learn more about the property simply go to the website, and all the relevant information is right there, quickly accessed.

Thus, when a potential buyer emails or calls Marc and Caroline, presumably she has already visited the Internet site and knows all about their house.

Finally, after some discussion, they list with a flat-fee MLS agent who called them from the site. For about $400, their home will appear on their local MLS.

Once their home is listed on the MLS, not only agents can view it. Their MLS listing soon appears on *www.realtor.com* and may also appear on other popular websites where buyers can see it.

Let's review the marketing that Caroline and Marc have generated.

- Images of the property (inside and out) are on the FSBO website.
- Asking price and terms are available both on the FSBO website and on other major websites.
- Location of the property is available to buyers.
- Size and configuration of the home (square footage, bedrooms and bathrooms, and so on) is available to buyers.
- All of the amenities, such as fireplace, large yard, fruit trees, oversize garage, and so on, are presented.
- The school district (and students' average test scores) is provided.
- Facts about local shopping, transportation, even crime statistics are offered.
- Buyers are given the opportunity to learn what comparable homes have sold for to evaluate the home's worth.

- The FSBO site offers buyers the chance to get pre-approved, so both buyers and sellers will know if the buyers qualify to buy the home.

In short, the Internet has allowed Marc and Caroline to use every marketing tool that an agent would use to spread the word about their home.

Further, because of all the information they've put out, potential buyers already know an enormous amount about their property before they even come to see it. In a sense, the buyers have been prequalified to purchase the home. Marketing is no longer a chance visit by a maybe buyer who comes knocking at the door. Now most buyers have full knowledge of what's being offered.

Unlike in the old days, Marc and Caroline when selling by owner are not operating alone and out in the cold. By finding buyers off the Internet and educating them about the home, Marc and Caroline have essentially done the sort of preparatory work that agents normally do. They've leveled the playing field, and as agents say, "They've got a hot prospect!"

Further, when a prospect does decide to buy, Marc and Caroline can go back to the FSBO site and get help with documentation, disclosures, inspection, reports, and almost everything else they need. The site may even be able to help them open an escrow account and run the closing.

Once again on the backside of the deal, the playing field has been leveled through the opportunities that websites offer buyers.

The Marketing Plan

Let's turn to specifics.

If you want to sell something, you have to come up with a marketing plan. Even if it's just lemonade, you still need a stand and a sign to attract customers.

Selling real estate is no exception. The professionals in the field know this well. Every good agent has a marketing plan. You need one too.

Many by-owner sellers mimic the marketing that agents use. For example, they put a big sign in front of their house and place ads in the local newspaper.

However, after that, the marketing plans of many by owners tend to fizzle out. Yes, you can create flyers and post them on your sign, on bulletin boards, and in housing offices of companies. All good ideas. But how do you generate the interest that agents can?

This brings us back to the Internet. Once you're on the Internet at a FSBO site and at an MLS site, how can you be sure potential buyers will see, stop, learn, and call?

Of course, a person trolling the Internet may just happen to spot your home, find it interesting, and give you a call. (MLS listings, unfortunately, frequently do not list the seller's phone number. But, they usually give the address, so a potential buyer can at least drive by and get the vital info from your sign.)

However, a good by-owner marketing plan involves more than just leaving it to chance that someone will happen upon your Internet-listed property. It involves *driving* buyers to your site. It combines both the features that the Internet offers and the groundwork you can do.

For example, instead of just listing your phone number on your sign and your flyer, why not also (or instead) list your home's Internet FSBO address? You'll drive buyers to your site, where they can learn so much more about your home.

Similarly, when placing a small advertisement in the local paper, why not list your by-owner website address?

In this way, you duplicate the synergy that agents get when they work together. Your plan uses the Internet to give yourself a marketing edge.

It's important to understand that you need a "clicks-and-mortar" approach. You need to make a visible target of your property on the Internet. But you also need to get out there physically and advertise, put up signs and flyers, and so on to drive those buyers to your site.

Marketing with Lots of Images

Everyone's heard the old adage, "A picture is worth a thousand words." Unfortunately, too few of us take it to heart when it comes time to sell our homes.

It's important always to keep in mind that buyers have little imagination. They have trouble visualizing anything they can't immediately see. And that includes the home you are advertising. You may write up a succinct, clever, and complete Internet ad, but even if buyers read it, they still may not have a good idea of what you're offering. On the other hand, one glance at a picture of the front of your home, and they will know precisely what you have to offer.

Real estate agents are well aware of this: they always include a picture with every listing, and they almost always include a picture with flyers they circulate (often attached to the For Sale sign in a small box). Too often, however, those who sell by owner overlook this obvious marketing tool and instead focus on the difficulty or cost of obtaining that picture. That's really a shame, because today it's incredibly simple and inexpensive to get a good image (or images) of your home for use both on flyers and for online listings.

Of course, you could use an old-fashioned film camera to snap a couple of pictures. You can have these scanned into a digital image at stores like FedEx Kinko's, after which they can be sent to your Internet site. Or you can send them to a website that will scan them for you.

A much better alternative, however, is for you to use a digital camera to obtain your image. You get an electronic file right away, and you can control better how the image looks. Today you can get a good digital camera, one that provides plenty of resolutions for your needs, for around $100.

Here are some tips for shooting your home for your website:

- Always include a front shot. Most cameras have trouble with wide angles, so back as far away across the street as possible. Try to take the shot when there are no cars in front. Try to shoot slightly up, as this angle will make the home look bigger.
- Shoot on a cloudy day. Strong sunlight will cast unwanted shadows on your home.
- If possible, include interior shots. The most important areas are the kitchen, living room, main bathroom, and master bedroom.
- Most digital (and film) cameras shoot too dark inside homes, but flash creates unwanted hotspots. Try to shoot without flash using natural light from open windows and with interior lights turned on. Increase the exposure on your camera, if possible. With digital images, adjust the brightness and contrast afterward on your PC using an image manipulation program, such as Photoshop.
- Use full-size digital images for creating flyers. Downsize your image to 50 KB or less for sending to the Internet.

When you run an ad in a local newspaper, your biggest marketing tools are the words *by owner.* You only need three or four lines to describe your home. A picture, of course, would be wonderful, but you won't want to pop for the hefty expense of including a photo in a newspaper ad.

When you list your home on an Internet site, a picture is the big hook. You can typically put up one to five images of your home. Use the one-two punch of a newspaper ad driving buyers to your online images to help put together a deal.

An Added Plus: Seller Financing over the Internet

Today most sellers expect buyers to pay cash. The reason, of course, is that great institutional financing is so readily available. Sellers expect that buyers will go to a mortgage broker and arrange all their financing so that when the offer comes in, it's "cash to the seller," even though it's financing to the buyer.

Most Internet FSBO sites make this simple by including a link to a mortgage company. Buyers simply click on the link and have the opportunity to get pre-approved. A lender looks over their financials and determines how big a monthly payment, and from that, how big a mortgage they can afford.

Unfortunately, expecting buyers to come in with all-cash offers overlooks an opportunity that could benefit sellers who have large equity positions—financing the sale themselves. Of course, this used to be very difficult for those selling by owner, especially with regard to coming up with the appropriate documents. However, , the Internet makes it easier.

Two potentially big benefits (as well as some perils) come with seller financing. The first is enabling a buyer who is having trouble getting traditional financing to buy your home. There's certainly a lot of them in a tight market. You might get a sale you'd not otherwise make to a buyer who might otherwise not be able to buy. It's a win-win situation.

Second, sellers with relatively large equity can often get a higher interest rate on their money through offering a mortgage to buyers than if they sold and stuck their money in a bank. Consider this example. If you have $100,000 in equity, sell your home, and bank that money, then at current rates, you'll be lucky to get 3 or 4 percent interest. On the other hand, offer financing to the buyer in the form of a mortgage, and you may get 6 to 8 percent interest.

Converting equity to a high-interest-rate-bearing mortgage is particularly appealing to more mature sellers who need the money for retirement purposes.

Most seller financing involves giving the buyer either a first or second mortgage. The order of the mortgage determines its risk, with a second mortgage being riskier than a first, hence usually commanding a higher interest rate.

The challenges of seller financing come in three areas:

1. Qualifying the buyers (to be sure they can make the payments)
2. Obtaining documents to create the financing (now available online)
3. Protecting against loss of all or part of the equity invested, if the buyer defaults

Why the Internet Makes It Easier

Qualifying buyers yourself these days is made simpler through the ready availability of credit scores (for example, see *www.myfico.com*). Borrowers can readily obtain these and then show them to sellers to woo their financing.

Further, the Internet can help with the sometimes complex documentation. Online services provide the tools to offer your own seller financing. Of course, it's always a good idea to have your attorney check over any documents before using them.

Unfortunately, sometimes buyers do default, and then the usual remedy to sellers is foreclosure. This, however, can be a difficult and expensive process, the fear of which often keeps sellers from offering financing.

Seller financing remains a potentially savvy way of getting your home sold *and* earning a higher interest rate on your equity. Consulting a financial planner and an attorney is always suggested.

Is It Really for You?

Remember what we discussed in the first chapter? Selling by owner may not be for everyone. Perhaps you're the sort who would rather call a plumber than fix a leaking washer? Maybe you'd rather hire a painter than paint your own closet? Or you could be the sort who would rather have a gardener than cut your own lawn.

If so, don't feel bad. (You'll just always remember the money you could have saved!)

However, if you're into saving money and aren't afraid of doing some work, then the Internet can provide you with all the tools you need. It can give you a great marketing opportunity. If you plan things out and use the resources it offers, it can also give you a great chance of success.

By using a "clicks and mortar" approach, you can quickly sell your home.

Still not convinced?

If you don't try, how do you know it won't work? Just think, today you might put up a sign that says "For Sale by Owner," and tomorrow you might hook a buyer!

It's happened. Sometimes it's as simple as your neighbor looking for an investment property, being attracted by your sign, and buying your house.

If you don't at least give it a shot, you'll never know if it could happen to you.

5 FSBO Your Way Out of Foreclosure?

IF YOU'RE FACING foreclosure, I'm sure you're desperately looking for a way out. Foreclosure can be devastating both financially and emotionally. I'm also sure that many people have given you suggestions about what to do to save your house and to save your credit.

In a sense, I'm going to do the same thing. However, in this chapter, I'm going to limit the topic just to the basics of foreclosure and how selling FSBO may be able to help. (For more information about handling impending foreclosure, try reading *Save My Home: 10 Steps to Avoiding Foreclosure* by Tom Geller, Kaplan, 2008.)

How Did I Ever Get Here?!

Almost no one expects to face foreclosure. Rather, it usually sneaks up on us when we're not looking and then tends to overwhelm us. Frequently people who are in foreclosure often don't really understand how they got there. When that's the case, it becomes even more difficult for them to get out from under.

Foreclosure typically comes about from three main causes:

1. We buy a property that's basically beyond our means and then can't keep up with the payments.

2. We have an adjustable-rate mortgage (ARM) that resets to a higher interest rate and higher payments that we can't afford.
3. Our income suddenly declines, such as when an illness prevents us from working.

The current enormous number of foreclosures has come about mainly from reasons 1 and 2 above. Many people stretched to get into properties that were really too much for them, hoping to resell quickly. When the market collapsed and this became impossible, they couldn't maintain the properties. (Speculators sometimes bought 10 or 20 homes hoping to flip them quickly, only to find they were stuck with the houses and 10 or 20 payments a month.)

However, an even bigger number of foreclosures have come about because of the poor practices of major lenders across the country. Endeavoring to help people get into homes (and to make more profitable loans), they created a relatively new kind of mortgage that turned out to be a monster. It went by various names but mainly was called an "option loan."

With an option loan, the borrower was allowed to make greatly reduced payments. The amount of interest that was due but not paid was added to the mortgage. Thus, the loans grew bigger instead of smaller. All was well as long as property values went up faster than the mortgage grew. *And* as long as the mortgage payments didn't rise. However, when the market collapsed, property values shrank instead of growing. Even worse, the mortgages reset after two or three years, and then the payments sharply increased.

The lenders typically had told borrowers that when the mortgages reset, they would be able to refinance or resell. That was true—when the market was going up. But when the market turned down, reselling became difficult (increasingly so because the mortgages often had grown bigger while prices were falling), and refinancing became next to impossible because the owners no longer had sufficient equity in their properties.

The results are an historically large number of foreclosures. Perhaps you got caught in that slide? If so, now the question becomes: how to get out?

Selling Your Way Out

When it becomes clear that you can no longer make your payments, the first option usually is to try to refinance to lower payments. As we've noted, however, that's increasingly difficult in a tight market. So the next-best option becomes selling.

Most borrowers faced with foreclosure do, in fact, try to sell their homes. Most list with an agent hoping for a quick sale. That, however, may be impossible because frequently they are "upside down."

In the trade, *upside down* means that the seller owes more than the property is worth. How does someone get upside down? It's not hard in today's market.

Getting Upside Down

Let's say you buy a home for $300,000 and you put 10 percent down ($30,000). You have a $270,000 interest-only mortgage, which at 7 percent interest should have payments of $1,575 a month. However, instead of making those payments, you opt to pay only $800 a month. In the case of your mortgage the interest you didn't pay (in this case $775 a month) is added to the loan balance. Your mortgage is fixed for two years, and during that time, a total of roughly $18,600 is added to your mortgage, bringing it to a total owed of $288,600.

Now the two-year fixed period is up and your mortgage resets. Suddenly you owe the full monthly payment, which now comes out to a whopping $1,684 a month, more than double your original payment.

Understandably, you can't afford this. So you decide to refinance to a lower monthly payment mortgage, such as the one you originally had before it reset.

Only in the last two years, the housing market has taken a dive. Your home is now worth only $290,000. Your equity has been reduced to $1,400!

You check with several lenders, but they all tell you that you don't have enough equity for a new loan and you don't have enough income to make your new high payments (as if you didn't know that!).

KEY CONCEPT *In our example of getting upside down, the borrower put 10 percent down. However, many lenders allowed borrowers to get in with nothing down. If that were the case, the situation would be over $30,000 worse!*

So you decide to sell. You contact an agent who explains that she charges a 6 percent commission. On a sales price of $290,000, that comes to $17,400. Plus, there will be roughly another $3,500 in closing costs, so that comes to about $21,000 in costs to sell your home.

But you only have $1,400 in equity. That means that to sell, you'll need to come up with about $19,600 in cash out of your pocket. This is called being upside down.

Sales price	$290,000	
– Reset loan amount	(288,600)	
– Agent's commission	(17,400)	
– Closing costs	(3,600)	
Total	**($19,600)**	→**Upside down!**

Obviously you can't sell using an agent, unless you're willing to throw in a lot more money (which most people aren't). So if you're like many borrowers in this situation, you throw up your hands and wait until the foreclosure process runs its course and the bank takes over your house, forcing you out not only with no cash but with ruined credit.

The FSBO Way

There is an alternative.

If you sell your home entirely on your own, as described in this book, you save the commission. Since that's the single biggest cost of selling, the savings are large. In this case, you'd probably save as much as $17,400, reducing your negative to only $2,200. You might indeed be willing to come up with this relatively small amount of money out-of-pocket to at least save your credit. By saving on the commission and by stretching, you can get out from under.

In the real world, however, things rarely work out so neatly. If it takes you two or three months to sell, that's two or three monthly interest payments added to your mortgage. At $1,684 a month, that comes to an additional cost of roughly $5,000 for three months. If it takes longer to sell, you're even further in the hole. (If you originally put nothing down, your hole is far deeper—about $35,000 more than what you could fetch on the property.)

Thus far, I'm sure that if you're in foreclosure, this seems all too familiar. Answers seem to offer hope but only result in costs that you probably can't handle. Being upside down is no fun.

Check with Your Lender

The next thing to do is to check with your lender. With so many properties in foreclosure, lenders are loathe to take any more back. Thus, they are looking for a way out. (Also, the federal government usually insists that they try to work something out with you.)

The lender may be willing to forgive a number of payments. Or it may be willing to add the payments to the mortgage balance. Unfortunately, while this may keep you temporarily out of default on the mortgage, it won't help with the sale, because it grows the mortgage balance.

However, checking with your lender and attempting to work out a solution is a very important first step, even if the results aren't what you hoped. The reason is that by talking, you establish rapport with the lender for the all-important next step.

Creating a "Short Sale"

When you're upside down, as so many people in foreclosure are, the simple truth is that there's not a whole lot you can do about curing the problem (short of putting more money in yourself, with you probably can't or don't want to do). However, there is another party who is in a position to cure the problem: the lender.

Understanding the Lender

We all know that lenders portray themselves as autocratic. When you need money, you come to them, and they dictate the terms. You either accept their terms, or you don't get the loan.

Similarly, when you can't make the payments on a mortgage, the lender dictates the terms of the foreclosure process. It records a "notice of default," which gives you a certain amount of time to pay up all back interest (and penalties) or it will foreclose and take your property away. It's all written in stone with no possibility of compromise…or even mercy.

At least that's the way lenders like to be seen.

However, there's another side of them that they don't like you to know about. That's the side that requires them to follow banking laws and stay solvent. When you face foreclosure, not only is it traumatic for you, but it's also a crisis for the lender.

When you make your mortgage payments on time, you're an asset to the lender. You contribute to its profit.

When you don't make your payments, you're considered a "nonperforming" loan. Suddenly you move across the ledger from asset to liability. The money that you don't send in each month now contributes to a loss.

What's worse, the government requires banks to put aside in capital reserves some money just in case you don't make up your payments and right your loan. Now, not only are you contributing to loss, but you're also tying up capital.

What's even worse, if you in fact do lose your home to foreclosure, the government now requires the bank to increase its capital reserves (to as much as 50 percent of the mortgage) in case there's a huge loss on your property (the bank can't sell it, either).

All of which is to say that not only are you desperate to get out from under, the bank is probably just as desperate to help you do just that.

Creating an Opportunity. However, if you simply throw up your hands and do nothing, there's little the lender can do, either. The foreclosure process will chug along until your property is sold by court order (in states that have judicial foreclosure, such as Florida) or by a trustee's sale (in states that have trust deeds, such as California). Either way, you—and the bank—both lose.

So what can you do?

The answer is that you can ask the bank to take a "short sale." That simply means you ask the bank to take less than it's owed by the terms of the mortgage. Instead of demanding $288,600 (in our example above), plus additional interest and penalties, you ask the bank to accept less.

Will the lender go along with a short sale?

Sometimes. Especially when there are lots of foreclosures happening and the bank is worried about its solvency.

How It's Done. Simple, right? You just ask the lender to take less, and everything works out okay.

Nope. Unfortunately, banks don't like to be thought of as patsies. If you use the logical, direct approach, you're likely to get a negative response. You have to be a little bit sly about it.

Usually the best way is to get a buyer. Find someone who is willing to buy your property for close to market price. Then present the lender with a choice. (Remember, you're already talking to the lender, so you've got a face and body to present your deal to.) Either the lender can accept a short sale and everyone gets out from under. Or the lender can refuse, you'll lose the property to foreclosure, and the lender will acquire a big liability and potential loss.

The FSBO Difference

When you lay all the facts out for a lender, often the choice comes down to how big a hit the lender will take. In our example above, it's nearly $20,000 when you've got the property listed with an agent. On the other hand, if you don't pay the commission, the hit drops down to only $2,200. If you were a lender, which short sale would you be more likely to accept? One that cost you $2,200? Or one that cost you $20,000?

In my experience, lenders don't like to see a real estate commission as part of the short sale. In many cases, they'll simply tell you no. They may even suggest you get out there and sell it on your own. Or pay the commission on your own.

The bottom line is that in my opinion, you increase your chances of getting a lender to give you a short sale (and thus bail you out) when you don't have to pay an agent's commission.

K E Y   P O I N T *Warning! You might owe federal and state income taxes on a short sale! The IRS may look on mortgage forgiveness (remember, in a short sale, part of the loan is "eaten" by the lender) as income to you. (The federal government was considering temporarily lifting this rule as of this writing. The rules are complex and beyond the scope of this book, so check with a good tax attorney or accountant.)*

Other Alternatives to Consider
Lease-Option

If you have the cash to make a few monthly payments, you may consider trying to sell your home as part of a lease-option. You find a tenant who's willing to pay above-market rent (part of which you refund to the tenant if they buy the property) and give the tenant both a lease on the home as well as an option to buy it at a predetermined time in the future.

Tenants frequently love lease-options, because these arrangements allow them to get into a property for basically rent. Sellers like them, because they get a higher-than-market rent with which to make mortgage payments—and they get out from under.

There are many pros and cons to lease-options as well as legal barriers. (Texas, for example, severely restricts a seller's ability to create a lease-option.) You should check with a good attorney before attempting it. Also look into my book, *Rent to Own*.

Deed "In Lieu"

Yet another alternative to consider is giving the lender a deed in lieu of foreclosure. In other words, you jump ahead of the foreclosure process. You contact the lender and propose that instead of going through the whole foreclosure process, the lender can save time and money by simply accepting a deed from you.

If the lender accepts, you give it a deed, move out, and get on with your life.

Why do this? To try to save at least some of your credit. When you lose a house to foreclosure, it's reported to credit bureaus and adversely affects your ability to get credit for years to come. With a deed in lieu, there is no foreclosure, so none appears on your credit report.

However, it's not home free, either. Most lenders will report to credit bureaus that they received a deed in lieu, and that *will* appear on your credit report. Your credit will still be affected, usually just not as badly.

Getting Out of Foreclosure

The year 2007 reported the highest levels of foreclosure in recent history, and 2008 may well surpass it. (Unfortunately, accurate records were not kept during the Great Depression.)

If you're faced with foreclosure, don't hide your head in the sand. Become proactive. Find out what you can do to save your home or, if that's impossible, at least salvage some of your credit.

6 | **Shape Up Your House**

IF YOU WANT to sell a car for top dollar, you'd better be sure it's in perfect running order *and* that it's been "detailed" inside and out. Otherwise, it will take forever to sell, and you'll get a greatly reduced price.

The same holds true with a house. To get top dollar and a quick sale, the house must be in perfect operating condition, and it must look sharp. In this chapter, we'll look into what needs to be done to shape up your home. In the next chapter, we'll see how to stage it to sell.

Shaping Up

Shaping up simply means repairing anything that's broken—returning your home to the condition it was in when it was brand new. (*Staging* means going a step further and working on the presentation, as we'll see in the next chapter.)

If your home isn't shaped up, buyers will think of it as a problem property, a house with a defined issue. For example, your roof leaks, and you don't fix it. Buyers will think of your home as "the one with the leaky roof." They'll worry about how much it might cost to fix the roof or perhaps replace it. If they even bother to make an offer, they'll begin knocking thousands, probably tens of thousands, off the price to compensate for the bad roof. As a result, you'll get much lower offers, when you get any at all.

The obvious solution? Fix the roof.

Here are some of the things you typically must do to make sure your home is properly shaped up for a sale.

If it's broken, leaking, or otherwise damaged, you need to do these things:

- Fix the roof.
- Fix the foundation.
- Fix any cracks in the walls.
- Fix any broken windows or screens.
- Repair any holes in walls.
- Fix any warped or sagging doors.
- Repair the heating and air-conditioning system.
- Repair any leaky or nonfunctional plumbing.
- Fix the light switches or light fixtures.
- Fix the appliances.
- Repair the driveway.
- Replace the front door along with its hardware.
- Repair any bad flooring.
- Fix any serious yard problems such as flooding, broken fences, or overgrowth.

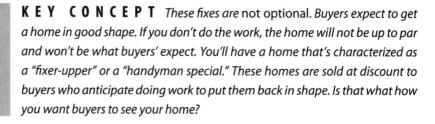

KEY CONCEPT *These fixes are not optional. Buyers expect to get a home in good shape. If you don't do the work, the home will not be up to par and won't be what buyers' expect. You'll have a home that's characterized as a "fixer-upper" or a "handyman special." These homes are sold at discount to buyers who anticipate doing work to put them back in shape. Is that what how you want buyers to see your home?*

Don't Overdo It

One of the problems I've had all my life is that I tend to move to the extreme. If I need an aspirin, I'll take two, since more is obviously better. If I'm fixing a toilet that's broken, I'll put in a new one, since that's better. When I do home construction and the house needs a 4" × 6" beam, I'll put in a 6" × 8". I've always had the habit of overbuilding, of overdoing the work.

I suspect that lots of other people feel the same way, and this tends to come out when it's time to fix up a home for sale. When fixing a cracked floor in the kitchen, why not put in a new kitchen? When fixing the broken air conditioner, why not replace it with a newer, bigger (and more costly) air conditioner?

The reasoning here is that by doing the additional work, by going the extra mile, you'll get a house that will sell for more and will sell quicker. But is that really the case?

Consider this real-life story of Jan and Jim.

Jan and Jim felt that their old-fashioned kitchen needed fixing. So they looked into replacing the scratched and sagging cabinets and found it would cost around $7,000; a new countertop to replace the existing one with cracked tile ran the total up to about $15,000. While they were at it, they thought they might as well put in a new stove, sink and faucet, garbage disposal, trash compactor, dishwasher, and built-in microwave. It would cost them about $25,000 to "fix" their kitchen.

When I talked with them about selling their home, I suggested an alternative, which they decided to do. Jim filled in the cracks in the cabinets' surfaces, rehung the doors, and then painted them. They had been a natural stained wood that was scuffed. Now they offered a bright, clean, painted look that was very modern. In addition, he repainted the rest of the kitchen and put in new light fixtures. He replaced the broken tiles on the countertop with "accent" tiles (tiles of a different color and appearance that added an accent to the countertop's appearance) and added new faucets, but he stayed with the old sink that was in good condition. They did add a new, modern stove and dishwasher but left the old garbage disposal, which worked, and did not add the trash compactor or the built-in microwave. The total cost was under $2,500.

Did it look as good as a totally rehabilitated kitchen would have looked? Certainly not.

Did it look good enough to sell the house? Certainly did.

K E Y C O N C E P T *You want to do fix-up work that is appropriate for the problem that you have. You don't want to "overkill" the problem. Don't spend more money than you can get back from selling.*

The same holds true for bathrooms and other rooms. When you're going to sell, spend the lowest amount that will give you a good-looking result.

Beware the "Hidden Systems"

One area of special concern is the "hidden systems." This includes plumbing, electrical, heating/cooling, and so on. What's important to grasp about these systems is that they *don't show*. When prospective buyers walk through your home, chances are they will give only a passing glance to your furnace, if they look at it at all. Buyers will just assume that it works.

That's why it pays to fix and not replace these systems. For example, it might cost you $350 to fix your furnace but $3,500 to replace. Yes, a replaced furnace will last longer and be more efficient, but it won't add $3,500 in value to your home. Except in very cold climates, where installing a high-efficiency furnace may make a real difference to a buyer, in most cases, buyers will simply grunt when you tell them of your expense in adding a new furnace. They won't pop for a dollar more in price. They'll just assume you had to do it to sell the house; it won't even occur to them that you could have just repaired the old one.

 K E Y C O N C E P T *The moral here is simple—fix, don't replace; repair, don't add on.*

"Necessary" Additions

Additions and enlargements are almost never necessary. They may make you feel good about your house, but chances are you'll never get your cost back when you sell. Don't do them unless a house simply won't sell because it lacks something that people demand. You would simply be throwing away money.

Of course, to every rule there's an exception. Maybe the kitchen is just too small. Or maybe there's no family room. Or maybe there's no fireplace.

Whatever the cause, to sell quicker and for a better price, you may have to add or enlarge. If that's the case, I suggest you either lower your price to the point where people will buy the property in spite of the defect or bite the bullet and do the work.

Keep in mind, however, that adding or enlarging is the costliest of all enterprises. It takes dollars, time, and great effort.

Should You Spend the Money or Simply Disclose the Problem?

Sometimes. You can sell a home where the heating or air-conditioning system needs replacement. Sometimes you can sell a house with a leaky roof.

Once you find a buyer, you can disclose the problem and negotiate to pay *part* of the cost of the fix. Sometimes with big ticket items, you can get away with a middle course.

Of course, it should go without saying that you must disclose the problem to a buyer. If you don't, you'll almost certainly end up with a very angry buyer and, perhaps, even a lawsuit down the road. That's something you definitely want to avoid.

However, once you explain the problem, you may be able to negotiate the cost of getting the problem properly fixed. For example, consider a roof. Your roof may leak. If your roof is more than 25 years old, chances are it needs to be replaced. However, a new roof can easily cost $10,000 to $25,000. Of course, you don't want to spend that kind of money, especially since you've probably only lived in the house a few years yourself. Why should you be responsible for the entire cost of the new roof?

Only old roofs look, well, old. Almost anyone can tell when they need to be replaced. In addition to leaking, often shingles are cracked or falling out, the color is stained or mottled, there may be mold or debris on the roof, and so on. Any decent home inspector will tell the buyer the roof needs to be replaced.

It's time for compromise.

Recently I sold a house that had a wood shingle roof that had deteriorated. It was leaking and needed to be replaced. A whole new roof would have cost around $10,000 to $15,000, but to fix just the areas that were bad with a guarantee of no leaks for a year would only have cost around $2,500. I disclosed the problem, and a home inspection confirmed it. But I didn't fix the roof prior to sale. Instead I offered to fix it.

However, the buyer I found wouldn't be satisfied with less than a completely new roof, which is typical of buyers. I explained that I was willing to spend only the $2,500 in repair work. We compromised: I gave him a $5,000 credit, which he then applied toward the $10,000 replacement job after the sale.

If I had gone ahead with the repair work, the buyer still wouldn't have been satisfied (because he wanted nothing less than a new roof), and I would still have had to negotiate a price concession. Not doing the work actually paid off.

A few years ago, I sold a home that had no air conditioning yet was located in a moderately warm area. The buyer wanted air conditioning for the summer months.

I explained that the house had been built without air and previous owners hadn't minded. The buyer wasn't satisfied, so I dropped the price an additional $1,000. Then the buyer was happy.

Negotiate Big-Ticket Items

The point here is that almost always, big-ticket items are negotiable. In the example above, new air conditioning probably would have cost me $3,500, but I negotiated a reduction of half what it would have cost me and made the buyer quite happy.

In most cases, it pays not to do big-ticket items but instead to point them out to the buyer and then negotiate an amount acceptable to all, which can be in the form of a sales price reduction. More often than not, this will be more acceptable to the buyer and will get you a quicker and even higher-priced sale.

Things Not to Do

Do *not* undertake the following projects to prepare your home for sale:

- Don't add a pool, spa, deck, or expensive shrubs to the backyard.
- Don't enlarge or add on unless it's to correct a defect in the house.
- Don't spend money on major replacement jobs that don't show, such as replacing a heating system. If something's broken, have it fixed instead.

Shape It Up

In truth, the best approach to fixing up your home is a pragmatic approach. While everything that's broken must be fixed, how it gets fixed—whether you repair, replace, or negotiate—is up to you.

For more information on shaping up your home, check out my book *Fix It, Stage It, Sell It—QUICK!* (Kaplan, 2007).

7 Staging Your Home for Sale

STAGING IS A relatively new term that's come into vogue during the past decade. It replaces older terms such as *dressing* or *fixing up* your home. It means giving your home a good presentation, showing it off to best advantage. It's based on the principle that what buyers see and like, they'll want to buy.

 KEY CONCEPT *Don't assume buyers will be able to visualize what your home could look like. They'll only see what it does look like.*

Buyers almost universally see only what's in front of them. They believe their eyes absolutely.

For example, your home may boast an absolutely smashing entry with tile floors, wood trim, solid oak doors, marble columns, and more, but if the floor, walls, and doors have been painted over with a dull paint, that's what the buyer sees—the dull paint, not the quality beneath.

Never mind explaining about the oak wood and tile and marble underneath. Ninety-nine percent of buyers won't pay any attention to you. All they'll see and remember is an ugly painted entry, and they'll probably dismiss your home as a possible purchase right away.

Even worse, let's say that you've got a wonderful home inside. Everything is neat, clean, well kept, and looks good, but you didn't get around to taking good care of the outside this year. The shrubs out front are wild because they weren't trimmed, and the front paint has weathered and has peeling patches.

Many buyers won't even bother to stop and look inside! Never mind that the inside of your home is beautiful. The outside will chill them and they'll drive on, never knowing what they missed. (It's called "curb appeal," or lack of it.)

Therefore, your first job is to give buyers something straightforward to look at. You must make your house appear smashing, wonderful, exciting, glamorous, even sexy. Don't let those buyers wonder about your place. Tell it all at a glance. Make your house look so splendid that even someone with 20/100 vision will turn around to admire it. In other words, leave nothing to the buyers' imagination, because they don't have any.

The Three *D*s of Staging

The basics of staging your home are really quite simple. Although you can now hire a "stager," typically for around a $1,000 in most communities, to come in and tell you what to do, you can actually do it all yourself with a little introspection.

I suggest beginning with the three *D*s of staging:

1. Declutter
2. Depersonalize
3. Deodorize

You want to make your home as desirable as possible to a buyer. Just doing these three things will go a long ways toward accomplishing that goal.

Declutter

Clutter is what happens as we live in a home over time. We begin accumulating things. A chair here, a table there, another couch. And especially trinkets. We may have a wise old owl statue on the fireplace mantle. We like it, so we acquire another owl for the kitchen. Then a few more for the living room. Pretty soon there are more owls in our house than people!

What to do with clutter?

As a general concept, I always advise people to take one-third of their furnishings and get rid of them. Move them out to another location, sell them, even give them away. If your goal is to sell your home quickly, then getting rid of your clutter is an important first step.

 K E Y   C O N C E P T *When your home is cluttered, buyers only see your stuff in it. They have trouble imagining where their things would fit. And if their things won't fit, why should they buy?*

Start with Your Furniture. Most of us have far too much furniture. When we first move in, we often have minimal furniture, just enough to get by. Then, as time goes on, we'll accumulate a piece here and there. There's the sofa that Aunt Sophie gave us and the table from grandma. Many houses act like giant magnets for clutter.

What's worse, most of us seldom throw out our old furniture. We become lovingly attached to it. The classic example came for me from that old television show, *Frazier*. Frazier had an ultramodern apartment obviously laid out by an interior designer—except for one decrepit old chair held together with duct tape that his father loved to sit in. The chair was an eyesore, yet it was a cherished piece of furniture (for his dad). Too often, our own homes are filled with such cherished eyesores. So many of them, in fact, that after a while, each room is overflowing with furniture. I've been in some homes where you can barely weave a path from one end to the other, they're so cluttered with furnishings.

Further, often even after we take out some of the furniture, what we have left is the wrong stuff. That's because few of us can afford to have an interior decorator come in and design our living space. For most of us, decorating is a matter of dragging our old furniture, accumulated over time, from our last home to our new home.

As a result, often the old furniture is simply too big to fit, the wrong style or color, or incredibly dated. Or perhaps we buy things on sale—a chair here, a chest of drawers there, a couch from someplace else. The best thing that can be said is that our mix of furniture is "eclectic." The worst is that it's a hodgepodge of styles, colors, materials, and pieces.

What to do? Get rid of everything that's mismatched and detracts from the room. If you're not sure, ask a few friends to be honest with you. Often having another pair of eyes gives a whole new perspective.

Don't Forget Your Clothing. Just as we tend to accumulate furniture, we also tend to accumulate clothes. When it no longer fits or is out of fashion or worn-out, do we throw it out? Or do we stuff it in the closet for that one occasion when we might need it?

Most of us do the latter, so most of our closets look like sardine cans with the sardines spilling out. And what does this tell a prospective buyer? It says that our house is too small and doesn't have enough storage space. After all, if our stuff is bursting the seams of the closets, how will they fit in their stuff?

Get rid of half of your stuff! Give it to charity, to your children, to the garbage collector. Your closets look right when you've only got enough clothes in them to fill half the racks. (And be sure to get rid of two-thirds of those shoes all over the floor of the closet!)

Don't Put It in Boxes! You need to get rid of clutter, not move it from one place to another. Don't put all your stuff in boxes and then stack those boxes, no matter how neatly, in rooms, in closets, or in the garage.

When you do, you're telling prospective buyers, once again, that your house is too small and doesn't have enough storage space. Rent a storage shed or store your stuff at friends' homes—anyplace but the house you're trying to sell.

Garage Clutter. Remember, people don't just buy your house—they buy your garage too. Too many tools laid helter-skelter, paint cans, rakes, boxes, and so on make the garage look stuffed, too full for a buyer's car and his own things.

Where Do I Get Rid of the Clutter? We've already suggested several ways. However, you should consider what I call the "rule of the whole." Pick and choose between what to keep and what to get rid of, and I guarantee you'll keep too much. On the other hand, simply say, "Toss it all!" and you've gotten past the indecision. Don't agonize over individual items. Just pack everything up and move it out. Here's a list of how you can get rid of clutter:

- *Throw it away.* Fill up a dumpster and haul it to the dump or pay a service to come and get it. Just get rid of it.
- *Sell it.* Remember garage sales? Just be sure you have them *before* you put up your home for sale—nothing distracts buyers like having a garage sale party in progress when they want to see your home. Also try CraigsList. com and eBay.com to sell more-valuable items.
- *Store it.* Rent a space in a miniwarehouse storage facility. Box up your clutter and haul it there. Later, after the sale, you can use it to clutter up your new home.
- *Give it away.* Many charities will come by and pick up your things (though not usually soft furniture, such as couches or mattresses). Not only are you doing a good deed, but you may be able to get a tax deduction as well. Also, consider giving things to your friends, associates, and relatives. Sometimes our discards can be useful to others.

KEY CONCEPT *Don't just move things around from one area to another. Moving stuff from the living room to the attic or from your bedroom to the basement doesn't help. You have to get it* off *the premises.*

Depersonalize Your Home

Nothing says *you* like your personal things. Photos, trophies, high school and college degrees, and so on make the house a home—your home. Unfortunately, that's exactly the opposite of what you need to sell your home.

You want buyers to visualize *their* things in your home. How can they do that when *your* things are everywhere?

Yes, it can be very hard to depersonalize a home, particularly when you're still living there. Nonetheless, it's necessary for good staging. You'll appreciate it when a buyer says, "Our family portrait will go perfectly there," in the space where your family portrait used to hang.

Here are some steps to depersonalizing your house:

- *Remove all family photos.* Any personal pictures have got to go. These include not only pictures of your family but also pictures of your car, your boat, or your dog. (Well, sometimes dog and cat photos can stay, since so many people like them.)

- *Get rid of trinkets.* We all have them. They're cups, clocks, mantle pieces, ceramics, glass pieces, and so on that we put on mantles, shelves, and virtually any other surface that holds them. They're special little things that we like, that say *us.* The trouble, of course, is that if buyers see so much of us in the house, they may have trouble imagining themselves in the house.

- *Remove your trophies.* They herald you and your family's successes. Great. But you don't want to impress your buyers—you want to sell them your house. Trophies are wonderful, and I fully applaud your desire to share them. Just don't share them with a buyer who wants to put her trophies in the same case.

- *Medicines.* So you take medicine on a daily basis. So do I. But don't leave the medicine containers out where buyers can see them. They add to clutter, and a buyer might think that it's a sick person's room. And nobody wants to move into a home where sick people used to live. (One way to derail any sale is to have a room in which someone not only was sick but died. When you disclose that, as you should, the whole sale may fall apart.)

- *Religious icons.* My suggestion is that you consider temporarily taking them down until you've got a sale. This is not to be antireligion. It's just that the person who may want to buy your home may be of a different faith, and a statement about your faith can unconsciously impact their desire to purchase your home.

Deodorize Your Home

Nothing will turn off a buyer faster than a noxious smell, whether it's rotten-egg smell, pet scent, or mold odors. Buyers pay attention to their noses. Just as with food, if it smells bad, it probably is bad. With so many homes on the market, why spend a minute more on a house that stinks?

Getting rid of odors, however, can be easier said than done. Here are some suggestions:

- *Pets.* Pet urine, especially that of cats, is the hardest odor to remove. This is not to say anything against cats. For most of my life, I have had pet cats. However, once their urine gets into flooring, it is impossible, in my opinion, to remove. (And I have tried every kind of deodorizer I could find on the market.) The only real solution is to remove carpeting, padding, and in many cases, wooden flooring! I've had some luck in getting the odor out of cement flooring, mainly by scrubbing, then laying down a coating of sealant, and then putting on a top floor.

  On the other hand, if your pet odor is limited to a litter box in just one room, remove that box and its contents and open the windows to air out the place. That may be enough.

  Though it may sound heartless, my suggestion is that you move your pet to a relative's or friend's home or even a kennel during the sales process. Just be sure to apologize to your pet for me.

- *Cleaning and solvent odor.* Household chemicals, such as cleaning agents and chlorine bleaches and ammonia, can leave an acrid odor that can burn eyes and bother the nose. Unfortunately, these tend to be the very chemicals that we use to clean up the house before showing it. Just be sure to air out your home for several days after using harsh cleaners and solvents.

- *Vacant house smell.* This is a peculiar odor so named because it's frequently noticed in vacant houses. Unfortunately, it can also be found in occupied houses.

  Typically it comes from mold and/or mildew somewhere in the home. You have to find where it's coming from and eliminate it. Once that's done, an airing out will usually get rid of the smell. (Look under carpets, on the floors of kitchen and bathroom cabinets, and anywhere in the home where moisture's likely to accumulate.)

Other Elements of Staging
Clean Everything

A clean home is not the exception when selling—it's what buyers expect. Anything less, and most buyers won't even consider making an offer, or if they do, will consider the home a "fixer upper" (though lack of cleanliness technically does not make it so) and make a highly discounted offer. Therefore, do yourself a favor and make sure that everything is spotless.

While this may seem obvious, it can be tiresome to accomplish. It's one thing to get your home up to speed with a clean-the-house drive on the day you first offer it for sale. It's quite another to keep it at that level for days, weeks, and sometimes longer while waiting for a buyer. Remember, that means that there can't be dishes in the sink or even the dishwasher, all carpets must be recently vacuumed, all clothes put away, and so on. Yet to sell FSBO (or even with an agent), it's what you must do.

In addition to the normal cleanup, here are some other areas of cleaning that you may want to consider taking on:

- *Walls.* What do you do about marks, scratches, and stains on walls? If the wall's been painted with a high-gloss paint, almost always the marks and stains can be removed with a good detergent cleaner and some elbow grease. Walls painted with a flat wall paint are a different matter, however. This paint can seldom be washed or cleaned. Any detergent or degreaser you use is likely to leave a mark. And scrubbing only removes the paint. My best suggestion is simply to repaint. It's not that expensive, and it's quite easy with modern latex-based paints that are low-odor and wash up with water.
- *Kitchen appliances.* How clean your oven is may determine how buyers see the cleanliness of your home overall. Also, clean the refrigerator, dishwasher, and any other kitchen appliances.
- *Bath and kitchen countertops.* Be sure that all dishes and pans are off the kitchen countertops. Use a mild detergent to clean stone or laminate. If you have tile, grout is often discolored by dirt. Try carefully scraping the grout with a bristle brush. A number of companies now make chlorine sticks that will bleach the grout white (not an option if you have colored grout). In extreme cases, have the old grout removed and have the tile regrouted.
- *Cabinets.* These tend to get food spilled on them, and the food often sticks. A quick wash with a good detergent, such as Fantastic of Simple Green, may be enough to bring them back to a shiny new condition. If not, restaining or repainting may be an option.

- *Wood or linoleum floors.* Wash and polish with a cleaner designed for the surface. For stone and wood, follow the manufacturer's or installer's directions
- *Windows and screens.* Clean them thoroughly with a mild soapy solution. Finishing off the windows with a glass cleaner may eliminate any smears. Also, replace worn or broken screens as necessary.

Special Treatment for Carpeting

When you first walk into a house, office, or any new building, your eyes tend to drift down. We all tend to look at the floor to make sure we don't trip.

What do we see? Is your wall-to-wall carpeting clean and new looking? Or is it dirty, worn, and frayed?

If it's the latter, it will make a big difference in a buyer's mind. Never mind pointing out that the buyer can replace the carpeting. You have to *show* buyers what the house will look like with fresh carpeting, not just ask them to imagine it.

My suggestion is to at least call in a professional carpet- and floor-cleaning service and have them do your house. Don't try to save money and do it yourself with a carpet cleaner you rent at a grocery store.

Professional services can make even an old, worn-out carpet look better. And in most cases, they can do it for a couple of hundred dollars.

On the other hand, if your carpeting is more than few years old or looks very tired, your best bet is to put in brand-new carpeting. Brand-new, inexpensive carpeting looks good for at least six months. It almost always looks a whole lot better than old, expensive carpeting, even if it's been cleaned.

How much does new wall-to-wall carpeting cost? Be aware that it's probably a lot cheaper than you think. With the development of new fibers, many types of carpeting are quite inexpensive today. If you need around 180 yards (typically enough for an 1,800-square-foot home), you can expect to pay anywhere from a low of about $3,500–$4,000, including installation, to a high that goes as high as you want to go. (It is possible to spend tens of thousands of dollars on really fine carpeting, although that's a waste in all but the most luxurious of homes.)

A quick additional word about carpet color. The rule is that the carpeting tends to look lighter when installed than when you look at a sample. When you're buying to live in the house, therefore, most people select darker carpeting. It doesn't show the dirt as much and it requires less cleaning.

On the other hand, when you're installing carpet to sell, the rule is to buy lighter carpeting. I have installed nearly white carpeting in homes I was preparing to sell. I wouldn't think of living in the house myself, because I'd have to take off my shoes all the time for fear of tracking in dirt. (For staging, putting transparent plastic on the floor preserves the carpet while buyers walk on it.)

Here's a case where you can take advantage of the buyer's lack of imagination. Buyers see the light carpeting and think how wonderful it looks, while not imagining all the problems it will cause when they have to live with it.

Repaint Every Painted Surface a Buyer Can See

It's something you can do yourself in a few weekends, and it's not expensive. Most importantly, it shows well (provided, of course, that you do a good job!).

After you've painted the front of the house and the entry rooms, I suggest that you continue to paint the rest of the house. The next rooms to paint would be the kitchen, the guest bathroom, and the master bedroom, and then all the other rooms.

Paint them from floor to ceiling and choose a neutral color. It's important that the color be a beige, white, or a light color of some sort, because many people are put off by stronger colors. I'd avoid strong blues, greens, and yellows. Yes, you may find a buyer who loves a specific color. But for each one of that kind of buyer, you'll come across 50 others who hate it. You have to play the odds and go with the most neutral colors.

By the way, if your house has an acoustical ceiling (sometimes also called a "popcorn ceiling"), popular in some parts of the country for the past couple of decades, and it's dirty, what do you do? Do you paint it?

You can. Except that it soaks up paint. It could cost you as much in time and money to paint an acoustical ceiling as it would to paint the entire rest of the inside as well as the outside of the house. (If you do paint, try first sealing it with shellac.)

My suggestion is that you hire a contractor to remove the ceiling. It's done by wetting it and then scraping. The contractor then tapes, retextures, and paints the ceiling, leaving it looking modern, clean, and neat.

The only problem is if your home was built prior to around 1978 when asbestos was used. While for a late-constructed home, acoustical ceiling removal isn't that expensive—often under $2,000 for an entire typical medium-sized house—with asbestos, the price skyrockets and can be as much as $10,000 or more. You should have your ceiling tested for asbestos before proceeding. (You can find a lab to do this online at sites such as *www.asbestostesting.com* or *www.sailab.com.*)

Repainting or removing an acoustical ceiling can refresh your house, help make it look new again, and make it far more saleable.

Repaint or Replace the Front Door. The first thing that anyone sees about your house, at least about the interior, is the front door. Thus, the quality of your front door makes the first, and a lasting, impression.

For this reason, I suggest that you at least give the front door a good coat of paint. On the other hand, if you want to really improve the appearance of your home, you may actually want to replace the door(s).

A new front door isn't that expensive at discount lumber stores. You can get a good one in solid birch or mahogany for around $500. For another $100, you can get it in oak. Add in the costs of stain, the hardware, and installation, and you can have a brand-new front door for around $1,000.

Seem like a lot of money? Not when you think of the impression it makes. A great-looking front door will knock the socks off potential buyers. I believe it returns far more than it costs in your ability to resell quicker and at a higher price.

Stage the Backyard

I don't think much of spending money on the backyard. My feeling is that the vast majority of buyers are not swayed one way or another by a backyard. Therefore, this is the last place I would spend money.

Of course, that doesn't mean you can leave the backyard a mess. Any buyer is bound to notice overgrown grass and shrubs, weeds, and broken lawn equipment or toys. (In the last chapter, we mentioned fixing anything seriously derelict, such as a broken fence or standing water.)

If all you have in the backyard is an overgrown lawn, then, yes, I would pay the kid down the street $20 to mow the lawn, but no, I wouldn't spend a dime more than that. If you have shrubs and trees that need pruning, I'd call a gardener to trim but not plant. If you've got a lot of broken items and junk in the yard, I'd call a garbage collector to get rid of the stuff and maybe a handyperson to get it straightened out. But I wouldn't do much more.

You may be asking: What about all the wonderful attributes a backyard can have, such as a sun deck, overhang to offer shade, spa, pool, flower garden, and other amenities?

All of these are often more of a headache than they are worth when it's time to sell. Let's take a swimming pool as an example. Today, to put in a decent-sized swimming pool with adequate decking and equipment could easily cost more than $40,000, but when it comes time to sell, can you get an additional $40,000 for the property? I think not.

Quite the contrary, many buyers specify that the house they buy *not* have a pool. They don't want the hassle of cleaning it and keeping up the chemicals. In short, you may lose as many buyers as you get by trying to sell a house with a pool.

But what about price? Won't buyers pay more for a house with a pool than for one without?

Marginally, yes. In parts of California, pool homes tend to sell for perhaps $5,000–$10,000 more, on average, when they sell, than houses without pools, but that's a far cry from the $40,000 it costs to put in that pool. (On the other hand, in some elite neighborhoods, a pool is almost mandatory to make your home competitive with others.)

If you have a house with a pool, make the best of it. Keep the pool spotless and well chlorinated—and hope that you find a buyer who's willing to buy with it.

If you don't already have a pool, bite your tongue every time you want to mention the idea of adding one. I've owned many properties with pools and still own one today, and I can assure you that I have received very little financial benefit from them. In fact, they have always been more of a headache than they are worth.

Beautify the House

This is the final step of staging. It means you may need to add lighting to brighten your rooms, bring in flowers to add color, and move furniture around (or switch furniture between rooms) to make the home appear more comfortable.

For this, you need panache. My suggestion is that you either call in a stager or an interior decorator or ask a friendly agent (typically one who's hoping to get a listing) for professional advice. Most homeowners who've lived in a home for a while themselves find it very difficult to get a new perspective on such things.

One thing that I find helps is to tour the model homes of builders. These have all been staged. See how the furniture is arranged, what kind of furniture is used, how flowers are used as accents, and even how colored throws, scarves, and tablecloths are strategically placed. Looking with a critical eye can give you a lot of hints.

Do the Least Expensive First

Once you decide what needs to be done to stage your home, consider the cost. Most sellers are immediately stopped by financial considerations. (Few sellers have a lot of money to spend.) Short of taking out a home equity loan, you probably think you can't afford to stage the old house the way it should look. Yes, you want to sell, but you don't want to bankrupt yourself doing it. Yes, you agree that you need to prepare the home for showing, but you just can't afford to do it all.

What You Must Do

My suggestion is that you take one step at a time. Begin by concentrating your efforts on what costs less but shows more.

This can be a tough concept for some people. The truth is, that which makes the biggest impression often costs the least to do. Let's look at a few examples.

You decide to stage your family room in a big way. It's going to cost $3,000 for a wall of new bookshelves, $1,500 for new carpeting, and $500 for great new window coverings. In short, you're looking at an expenditure of about $5,000.

But, you say to yourself, think of what I'll get when I sell. Right?

Wrong. Chances are that your work in the family room, admirable though it may be, won't get you a quicker sale or a higher price—perhaps not a dollar more. In short, while you'll be spending a lot of money, to say nothing of time and effort, you'll be getting virtually nothing financial in return.

When a buyer comes in and oohs and ahhs about your redone family room, that person is really saying silently, "What an idiot that seller is to waste all that money on the family room. Of course, if I buy, I'll enjoy it, but why should I pay a dime more for it?"

Or another example: Your backyard looks like a toxic dump site. So you haul in sand and topsoil, build a deck and overhang, plant shrubs and flowers, and put in a small pond with a couple of fish. In short, you transform that toxic dump site into scenic park land.

Now any buyer's going to be knocked over backward upon seeing your yard and will rush in to pay more to buy the property, right?

Wrong!

Ninety-nine percent of buyers love a great backyard but won't pay ten cents more for it. It won't compel them to buy any quicker, either. They'll look at the front yard and the house and take away a first impression, and if that's good, then they'll think about the backyard and add it in as a free plus.

In short, all that time, money, and effort spent on the backyard gets you a passing nod, but it doesn't make your house that much more salable.

I realize that this may fly in the face of what you have been told about selling, but I believe it to be the truth. What gets a buyer's attention is the first impression, and what makes a good first impression usually does not cost much. Indeed, good first impressions are often made by simple cosmetic changes.

Think of the old Hollywood sets. Remember, they used to have entire cities that were nothing more than breakfronts. They consisted of the front of a building held up with posts with no sides, back, or top, but when we watched the movie, the place looked authentic; it looked convincing; it made a strong, believable impression on us.

The same holds true for your house. The truth is that what you need to do is the cosmetic work. It's not expensive, and it will make a big difference in terms of getting you a quicker sale and a better price.

The Under-$500 Staging

If you want to know what to do to prepare your house for sale effectively, here's a short list:

- Mow the front lawn, water it, fertilize it, and get it to look great. Cost: $50
- Plant new shrubs in front and trim old ones. Plant colorful flowers near the entrance. Clean the driveway and any cement paths. If the entrance walk is broken or damaged, pull it out and replace it with inexpensive stepping stones. Make the front look terrific. Cost: $250–$300
- Paint the front of your house. Use a good paint and a separate trim paint. Do an especially good job on the front door. Use a neutral color. Cost for paint: $50
- Paint the inside entry of your home as well as the living room, dining room, and kitchen. Use a neutral color. Cost for paint: $50
- Take a third of the furniture in your house and store it someplace else, preferably off the property. Put it in a relative's or a neighbor's garage. Cost: $0

Total cost:

Front cleanup	$ 50
Entry fix-up	250
Front painting	50
Inside painting	50
Furniture removal	0
Total	**$400**

In short, for under $500, you can dramatically improve any buyer's first impression of your property. By so doing, you will automatically increase your chances of a quicker sale and a higher price.

KEY CONCEPT *You can't rely on the buyer's imagination. You have to transform what the buyer first sees from something that's poor or mediocre to something that looks great. When that buyer walks in, he won't have to imagine what your house could look like if this were mowed or that were trimmed or the other were painted. It will be spelled out for him—no imagination required. Instead of a hard-to-read book, you'll give the buyer an easy-to-view movie. Instead of what "could be," you'll be showing "what is." Instead of "maybe," your buyer will be thinking "yes!"*

Furniture Considerations When Staging

Before moving on, an additional word about moving out some of the furniture. You may be wondering why I keep emphasizing this. The reason is that it's one of the most important things you can do to stage your home.

So here we go again: the big truth is that buyers want spacious houses. Yet most of us make our houses look small by cluttering them with too much furniture. If the interior design of your home was directed, like mine, by what's in your pocketbook, you bought what furniture you could find when it was on sale. That means that your house has an eclectic style: a little of this, a little of that. You bought what you wanted, what you liked, what felt comfortable to you, and mostly what was affordable. As a result, total strangers with totally different likes and dislikes who walk through will probably think that the place looks more like a den (as in animal) than a presentation. They will undoubtedly wonder at your taste, which simply means it's different from their own. Most of all, instead of remembering how spacious your place is, they'll recall it as a jumble of crowded, uncoordinated furniture.

How do you avoid this? Remove at least a third of your furniture. Just be arbitrary about it.

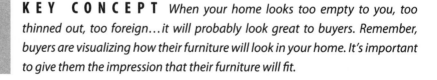

KEY CONCEPT *When your home looks too empty to you, too thinned out, too foreign…it will probably look great to buyers. Remember, buyers are visualizing how their furniture will look in your home. It's important to give them the impression that their furniture will fit.*

Do Expensive Things Too

I am not suggesting that you do only inexpensive, cosmetic things—just that you do those inexpensive projects first. As time passes and no buyer materializes, you may want to move forward with more expensive, material improvements. Again, these should be undertaken only after you've first done the inexpensive, cosmetic stuff.

Let's take a look at another example. Helen and Peter have owned their home for seven years. They've decided to sell FSBO. So they staged their property. They cleaned and trimmed the front yard and painted the outside front as well as the entry and big rooms inside. They thinned out their furniture, added light fixtures, cleaned the inside, shampooed the carpet, and more. In short, they did all the cosmetic, inexpensive things.

Now it's been a couple of months, and although they've had some nibbles, there hasn't been a buyer ready, willing, and able to purchase the property. The housing market isn't good in their area, and there are few buyers. Helen and Peter are beginning to think that they need to do more to improve the appearance of their property. What should they do next?

My suggestion to them, and to you, is to check around the neighborhood to see if there isn't something that the other homes for sale have that yours doesn't.

In Peter and Helen's case, all the other homes had two bathrooms while their house only had one. That was the deal stopper. No one was making an offer because of this drawback. Their choices? Give buyers a big discount on the price to compensate or add another bathroom. (They discounted their home, and it quickly sold.)

Or perhaps you have an older home, and all the other homes for sale nearby have modernized kitchens while yours has the original kitchen. Buyers simply don't like what you have to offer. The solution? Modernize the kitchen or, again, give a big discount.

These are *expensive* solutions. Don't do them first. Consider them only as a last resort. But if there's a problem that's keeping your house from selling, at some point, you may have to bite the bullet and do the work or drop your price.

Home-Staging Checklist

We've looked at many things you can do to stage your home for sale. Here's a list of some of them to help you get started.

For additional help on staging your home, check into my book *Fix It, Stage It, Sell It—QUICK!* (Kaplan, 2007).

Home-Staging Checklist

- Mow the lawn and keep it mowed.
- Replant grass in bare spots and fertilize lawn.
- Trim all the hedges.
- Plant colorful flowers in bare spots.
- Clean off driveway/remove oil stains.
- Clean/fix front walkways.
- Paint front of house.
- Paint front door(s) or replace it (them).
- Replace broken screens/windows in front.
- Paint entry and living rooms (such as entry, living room, family room, etc.).
- Remove a third of the furniture in the house. Don't store it in the garage; leave it at a relative's or neighbor's home or put it in a rental space area.
- Paint the entire inside of the house.
- Clean or, if possible, replace all carpeting throughout the house.
- Clean or, if possible, refinish all bare flooring.
- Increase the lighting by adding new light fixtures.
- Paint sides and rear outside of house.
- Rearrange the furniture (check out builders' model homes for ideas).
- Add colorful flowers, throws, scarves, and other items to beautify the home.
- Keep it spotless during the showing period.

8 Pricing to Sell

THE TROUBLE WITH FSBOs, as many buyers have discovered, is that they are often priced too high.

Many FSBO sellers are under the mistaken impression that because they are selling the property themselves, they can command a higher price than an agent-listed property. Indeed, often sellers will stubbornly list with themselves for a price that agents have already told them is too high.

Putting your property up for sale at an unrealistic price is the worst mistake you can make, whether listing with an agent or by owner. In today's market, buyers are extremely price-sensitive. Unless they perceive that the price is right, they won't even bother to give your property a second glance. Why should they with so many others for sale out there?

Let's face it, the big reason that most FSBOs don't sell is price. If you want to sell quickly, particularly in today's market, you have to give buyers an attractive price. Otherwise, your house will languish on the market while other similar homes more carefully priced sell.

KEY CONCEPT *A good lesson here is to go into the corner of the room and repeat to yourself: Price! Price! Price!*

Why do most FSBO sellers set their prices too high to attract prospective buyers? The seller is often focusing on the wrong goal. What you, the seller, should be most interested in is selling your property. What often happens, however, is that a homeowner who decides to sell without an agent begins focusing on two other things: how much he wants for the property and how much he can save by not paying an agent's commission; in other words, having more money in the bank. The seller ends up with unrealistic expectations of getting a fabulous sale and saving money in the process. The end result is a house that's priced higher than comparable houses and no offers from buyers.

Try to Price Just Below the Market

Here's a second pointer to remember. For most buyers, a FSBO is a *less desirable* home on which to make an offer than a listed property. This may seem to fly in the face of the longstanding arguments saying that buyers prefer FSBOs.

It's quite true, for example, that when you place your ad in the newspaper, the most compelling words you can write are "By Owner." That's almost guaranteed to catch buyers' interest.

What's never mentioned, however, is why buyers are drawn to FSBOs. The reason, quite simply, is that they are looking for a bargain. They know that agents are unlikely to show them your house; hence, they want to check it out to be sure that they're not missing out on anything good. They also realize that you're not paying a commission to an agent and hope that you'll pass on all or at least some of the savings to them.

When they discover that your house isn't any cheaper and, in fact, may be more expensive than others they have looked at, they will almost always drop you like a hot potato. Buyers don't really want to haggle with you. If it doesn't cost any more, they'd rather have the insulation of dealing with an agent rather than an owner.

Furthermore, the minute they walk into your house and realize you're not offering it for less, they'll assume that the real reason you listed is to save the commission an agent would charge for yourself, not for them. And if you're actually asking more than the market price, buyers will believe the real reason is that you refuse to accept what the market will bear for your home: you're a stubborn seller.

Either way, you'll be branded as an unmotivated and difficult person to deal with. In short, buyers won't want to deal with you. Why should they, when they can deal far more easily through an agent on a lower-priced listed home?

Buyers Find It Easier to Deal with Agents

Although we've touched on it, let's stop for a moment to consider this: the real reason most buyers feel uncomfortable dealing directly with the seller is confrontation. Buyers may hate the way you've arranged the backyard, but they don't want to tell you because they're afraid they'll offend you. They won't, however, hesitate to tell an agent who is representing the owner.

As we've noted, they may think that your home is way overpriced. But they don't want to argue with you about it. They'd rather smile and say how lovely your home is, then move on. But with an agent, they would definitely argue price. And the agent may convince them to make a lowball offer, which could get negotiations started.

K E Y   C O N C E P T *Agents love FSBOs. One would logically think that real estate agents would be afraid of FSBOs. After all, they represent competition. The opposite is actually true. Most agents love to see FSBOs for two reasons. The first we've already mentioned: FSBOs are often priced higher than competing homes. Hence, wise agents sometimes encourage buyers to stop by FSBOs for comparison. Some agents even accompany their clients to FSBOs so that the prospective buyers can see for themselves, by comparison, just how good the agent's listed deals are. The other reason is that FSBOs are an excellent source of listings. Agents know that a FSBO priced much higher than comparable homes in the area won't sell. Eventually the seller will get tired of showing the property, waiting endlessly for a buyer who never appears, and list.*

In short, most buyers dislike even the suggestion of a confrontation with a seller. That's why they prefer to talk to an agent.

Overcoming the Buyer's Resistence to Dealing with a FSBO

Basically, when you sell FSBO, you have to overcome a buyer's resistance to dealing directly with you. Given two identical houses located side by side, both offered at the same price but one a FSBO and the other listed with an agent, most buyers will prefer to deal with the agent's listing.

 KEY CONCEPT *The golden rule of pricing when you sell FSBO is that, since you're presumably saving on the commission and have some room to play with, give the buyers the price discount that they want. If you do, you'll sell your house faster and net more money.*

The question becomes, how do you overcome buyers' resistance to dealing direct? The quickest answer is offering a lower price. The mistake that most of those who sell FSBO make is thinking that they can keep the whole commission savings for themselves and sell quickly. You can't refuse to share the savings and realistically expect to sell the property in short order.

It all comes back to goals. Is your goal to save money? Or is it to sell your property quickly? If it's to sell your property quickly, you have an excellent chance of succeeding as a FSBO, because you're in a position to offer it for less.

Let's consider the following example. You've investigated the area (as explained later in this chapter) and found that homes just like yours are usually listed for around $200,000. You also discover that three properties have sold in the past six months for an average price of $190,000. That means that buyers are typically purchasing for 5 percent less than the listed price.

You also discover that the average commission charged in your area is 5 percent. (As noted, the amount of commission charged by an agent is always negotiable; most run from 4 to 7 percent.) On a $190,000 sale, that amounts to $11,400. Those sellers who sold for $190,000 actually netted out $178,600.

Now, how much do you ask for your house?

Many FSBO sellers would ask at least $200,000. Many would ask a higher amount, figuring that their house, with its "unique qualities" (every house has unique qualities) is worth more. They hope to save the difference between what the other sellers netted and their own asking price.

The problem, of course, is that you'll take forever to sell that property if you price it at $200,000. You probably won't even get offers. Buyers today are savvy and do their homework. They know that properties in your area are actually selling for $190,000. With an agent asking $200,000, they might make a lower offer. But, they probably will be hesitant to come to you and make that same lower offer. Remember, many buyers are hesitant to negotiate face to face.

But, what if you price your property at, say, $185,000? That's $15,000 less than the price of listed houses. Will you get offers? You bet you will. Buyers who might otherwise pass because of the inconvenience of dealing directly with a seller, all else being equal, will stand in line to deal directly with you and even pay full asking price, if they can save $15,000.

Of course, if you sold at $185,000, you would still net $6,400 more than comparable sellers who sell at $190,000 and pay a commission. Even if you had to accept a lower offer, say $178,600, exactly what other sellers had netted after a commission, you'd still be far ahead.

Why? Because your house would sell more quickly, and time is not only money—it's also peace of mind.

You Can Sell for More

On the other hand, you *can* sell your house for more, *if* you're willing to wait. It's a fact that by-owner sellers, if they are willing to keep their house on the market longer than listed properties take to sell, often do get a higher price.

A broker friend of mine describes an experiment she did at a meeting of real estate brokers to help determine a home's value. At this meeting, the brokers each stood up and touted one of their homes to the others, hoping that by doing so, they might discover another broker who had a buyer. When my friend stood up, she described a home that was listed for $250,000. When she was done, she asked the assembled brokers, over a hundred of them, "Does anyone have a buyer for this house at $250,000?" When no one replied, she asked, "Does anyone have a buyer at $240,000?" Again there were no responses. "What about at $230,000?" A few brokers raised their hands, tentatively indicating they might have clients who could be interested.

"At $200,000 would any of you yourselves be interested in the house?" A lot of hands went up. The brokers themselves were interested in buying at that price.

Investment Value

What the above story illustrates is how price functions when a house is considered strictly as an investment. Keep lowering the price, and you will eventually find an immediate buyer. I call this determining the commodity or the investment value.

Shelter Value

What the above example does not take into account is shelter. At the meeting my friend described, she was just testing to see how much she could get for that house if it were sold then and there. If the price got low enough, there were lots of takers, homebuyers as well as brokers, who would buy figuring they could flip it at a profit.

You'll always get plenty of buyers at fire sales or going-out-of-business sales, but prices have to be very low to attract them. On the other hand, if my friend had been willing to wait, she probably could have gotten buyers at a higher price.

If you're willing to wait, you will eventually attract buyers who want to live in the property. You hope that these shelter buyers will show up, fall in love with your house, and pay more for it than an investor would. This is the shelter value.

The shelter value is what a house will bring when it is for sale over time, say 90 days in a good market, 180 days in a bad one. The shelter value is usually the highest amount you can get for your home. (That's why when you're selling FSBO, you want to cater to buyers who plan to live in the property as opposed to investors who are looking to resell for a profit.) When it comes time to price your home, therefore, you'll undoubtedly want to get the highest shelter value. However, to do so takes time, and you'll have to determine how long you're willing to wait.

Remember that shelter value does not necessarily mean that you can get what you may feel your house is worth or what you have put into it. Shelter value is the highest price that you are likely to get by putting the house up for sale and then waiting for someone who wants to buy the property and live in it.

 KEY CONCEPT *You can usually get a higher price if you're willing to wait. If you want to sell sooner, you'll have to lower the price so the house sells more for investment than for shelter value.*

You Can Sell Quickly

You must be clear as to whether selling quickly is your goal. Are you interested in selling that house as quickly as possible so that you can get on with your life? Or are you interested only in saving money on the costs of the sale? If you are interested in a quick sale, you have the perfect opportunity with a FSBO, because you can offer to sell for so much less than you can by going through an agent. If you're willing to wait indefinitely, chances are you will get more money, but you'll be married to that house for a long time.

However, you may be interested in doing both, selling quickly and saving money. Again, you're in a great position to do this, because you can still discount your house for, say, as much as you'd pay for half a commission and still make it attractive to buyers. It might take a bit longer to sell than it would with a deep discount, but the result could still be a successful sale.

What Is Your Home Really Worth?

Now that we have the strategy in mind, let's see if we can put it into practice. Let's turn to the process of discovering just what the market for your home is.

Most of us loosely track housing values in our neighborhood. Anytime a nearby house sells, we usually try to learn the sales price. After all, that lets us know what our house might be worth.

However, for many of us, this process is selective. When we learn that a nearby house has sold for more, we add to the value of our house. However, when prices decline and a nearby house sells for less, we tend to dismiss that lower sale as market aberration. In other words, most of us add value when the market goes up but don't subtract value when the market goes down. Therein lies a trap that could keep you from selling your home.

The truth is that the market doesn't care how much you paid for your home; how much money, how many tears, and how much sweat you put into your home; how much you owe on your mortgage; or even how much your home was worth a year ago. All that the market cares about is what a buyer is ready, willing, and able to pay right now, today.

That statement can be very sobering, whether you sell with or without an agent. What it means is that your ability to sell in today's market is often linked directly to your ability to forget what you think your house is worth and instead sell for what a buyer will actually pay.

How Much Should You Ask for Your House?

Having noted the many considerations in determining price, let's now see just how much you can reasonably ask for your house. The estimating sheets in this chapter are designed to help you compare your house to other, similar homes that are for sale as well as those that have recently sold. By comparing it to similar homes, you'll come as close to knowing the true market value of your own home as anyone can, including brokers and appraisers.

The Comparison Method

There are many methods of determining the value of property. For example, an appraiser can use the cost approach, which bases price on cost of reproduction. Investment property is valued by the return on capital it makes. Most residential property, however, is evaluated on the basis of comparison. Find out how much a comparable property sold for, and that's the most likely value of yours.

Comparison is the method the mortgage appraisers, agents, and others involved in real estate use most often to determine the true value of a home. I suggest you use it too.

The comparison method is really quite simple, in theory. All you do is find four or five houses just like yours in your neighborhood that sold over the past six months, determine their sales prices, average them out, and that's what your house is worth, less trends in the market when it's declining.

In practice, however, the procedure can be a bit more complicated. The central problem is that sometimes it's hard to find good comparables.

There may be few sales in your area. Your house may be unique, or there may be few models like it. Sales prices themselves may be skewed by seller financing, cash-down sales, or other considerations.

To find out, the quickest way is to check for comps on the Internet. Many FSBO websites offer a source of them.

 K E Y   C O N C E P T *You usually can get a quick, free estimate of your home's value by checking* www.zillow.com *or another such website. For a nominal fee, many other sites will create a complete report on value for you.*

Getting an Agent to Help

Alternatively, you can check with a local agent.

You can explain to an agent that you're going to sell FSBO now. But if the property doesn't sell over time, you may list it with an agent. Most agents will be happy to help you in the hopes of getting your listing.

Ask for a comparative market analysis (CMA). All agents should know what this is. Using the computer system available to most offices, they can quickly punch up a list of comparable sales in your area and give you a quick analysis.

Do It Yourself

You can easily do your own CMA. (See the comp sheets at the end of this chapter.)

Of course, you'll want to double-check to be sure the comparables are truly similar to your home. If you can't find good comparables, then you'll have to do some fancy adjustments. If you find a house that's bigger or fancier than yours and sold for more, you'll have to guess how much less your house is worth. If you find a tiny, mousy house, much smaller than yours, you'll have to guess how much more yours is worth.

In the end, add up all your comparables and average them out. Be sure to separate the price asked from the price sold. Sold prices, not asking prices, are the true values. Also, try not to use sales more than six months old. Those older than six months may not reflect current market conditions. Voila! If you've done it correctly, you now should have a good idea of what your home is worth.

Following are the similarities to look for when selecting comparables:

- Same area of town and similar age
- Same number of bedrooms and baths
- Roughly same square footage
- About same style and design (e.g., not Victorian when yours is ranch)
- Roughly same amenities (e.g., has a pool if yours has a pool, has a fireplace if yours has a fireplace)

Compensating for Market Conditions

Finally, once you have your price based on comps, you *must* compensate for market conditions. When prices are rapidly rising, I always recommend adding up to 5 percent more, just so you don't leave anything on the table.

When prices are falling, you should cut your price by as much as 5 percent so you'll get ahead of the curve.

When prices are falling, buyers are worried that they will pay too much. They know that the house they buy today will be worth less tomorrow. You have to cut your price to tomorrow's value to reassure them.

 K E Y   C O N C E P T *In a falling market, sellers who cut their prices and get ahead of the curve typically sell within a few weeks. Those who don't can take upwards of six months or even much longer to sell.*

Comp Sheets

Figures 8.1 and 8.2 are a couple of comparable estimating sheets. You may want to duplicate them if you need more.

Figure 8.3 is a master sheet on which to make your final calculations. To use the Master Comparable Evaluation Sheet, enter the sales price of comparable properties. Then, using the Comparable Estimating Sheet, add an amount for homes that are worse than yours and subtract an amount for homes that are better than yours. Average the figures, and you'll have an average sales price and an average comparable price. If you've done your work carefully, the average comparable price should be very close to the market value of your home. Note: the difference between the list price and the sales price, you'll know how much of a discount buyers are currently getting.

Fig 8.1 Comparable Estimating Sheet (1)

Address_____

Square Footage_____

Style_____

Condition_____

Bedrooms	Number_____	
Baths	Number_____	
Family Room	Yes _____	No _____
Garage?	Yes _____	No _____
2-car	Yes _____	No _____
3-car	Yes _____	No _____
Pool?	Yes _____	No _____
Spa?	Yes _____	No _____
Fireplace?	Yes _____	No _____
Hardwood floors?	Yes _____	No _____
Air conditioning?	Yes _____	No _____
Good front yard?	Yes _____	No _____
Heavily traveled street?	Yes _____	No _____
General	Yes _____	No _____
Same neighborhood?	Yes _____	No _____
Same style?	Yes _____	No _____
Same amenities?	Yes _____	No _____

List Price $_____

Sales Price? $_____

Fig 8.2   Comparable Estimating Sheet (2)

Address_____

Square Footage_____

Style_____

Condition_____

Bedrooms	Number_____
Baths	Number_____
Family Room	Yes _____ No _____
Garage?	Yes _____ No _____
2-car	Yes _____ No _____
3-car	Yes _____ No _____
Pool?	Yes _____ No _____
Spa?	Yes _____ No _____
Fireplace?	Yes _____ No _____
Hardwood floors?	Yes _____ No _____
Air conditioning?	Yes _____ No _____
Good front yard?	Yes _____ No _____
Heavily traveled street?	Yes _____ No _____
General	Yes _____ No _____
Same neighborhood?	Yes _____ No _____
Same style?	Yes _____ No _____
Same amenities?	Yes _____ No _____

List Price $_____

Sales Price? $_____

Fig 8.3 Master Comparable Evaluation Sheet

	Sales Price	Add/Subtract	Adjusted Comp Price
House #1	$_____	$_____	$_____
House #2	$_____	$_____	$_____
House #3	$_____	$_____	$_____
House #4	$_____	$_____	$_____
House #5	$_____	$_____	$_____
House #6	$_____	$_____	$_____
House #7	$_____	$_____	$_____
Average sales price	$_____	$_____	$_____
Average comp price	$_____	$_____	$_____

9 Advertising That Draws Buyers

YOU NEED TO get the word out. Nobody will buy your home unless they know it's for sale. And they won't know until you tell them.

You may be living anywhere from a town that has 5,000 people in it to a city with a million or more. No matter where you live, however, there will always be a few buyers for your home. The trick is getting to those few.

How do you distinguish just the few who will purchase your property from all the others? To get to those few people who might really be buyers for your home, you may need to wade through thousands who aren't. To put it another way, you need to get your message to as many people as possible in the hope that a few of them will be the right ones. You accomplish this by publicizing and advertising your property in as wide a variety of media as possible. You do whatever you can to get the word out.

This need not be expensive. You can start by listing your home on a FSBO website, such as Owners.com or FSBO.com or any of the hundreds of other by-owner websites. This gets information about your property out there. You will also want to consider a flat-fee MLS listing (described initially in chapter 1 and detailed in the next chapter). That should help to get you exposure on Realtor.com and many other sites. In addition, you'll want to do all of the following things.

Get a Sign

A sign on the property can be the single most powerful advertising tool at your command. It lets everyone in the area know your home is for sale. (After all, how else might you discover that one of your neighbors is interested in buying your home?) The sign also allows anyone driving down the street to learn that your home is for sale. And when you advertise and people call and ask for directions to your property, you can simply direct them to your street and, when they get close, the sign will bring them right to your home.

Can I Build My Own Sign?

Anyone can put together a sign, but it takes a bit of knowledge to build a sign that snares potential buyers. Here's what to do.

To begin with, don't buy a ready-made sign at the store for a couple of dollars that says "For Sale by Owner" and gives you a place in which to write in your phone number.

These cheap, ready-made signs look just that: cheap. Potential buyers driving by are likely to think that you are a rank amateur, may not be very serious, and probably don't know much about what you are doing. After all, if you're not even willing to get a decent sign, how committed can you be to selling the property on your own?

Get a professionally made sign. A good Internet site will offer these, usually for a nominal amount of money. They will be catchy to attract a buyer's attention. And they will give not only your phone number but your Web address as well.

How do you know a good sign? It will look similar to an agent's sign. It will be roughly the same size (20" × 30"); the lettering will be clear and in a highly visible color, such as red; and it will be well designed and not look amateurish. The sign should also contain the following vital information:

- *FOR SALE.* Builders, landscapers, and politicians put signs in yards. You want people to know that in your case, it's the house that's for sale. These words and your phone number should be the largest elements.
- *BY OWNER.* This may be your best selling point. It doesn't have to be large, but it should be prominent.

- *PHONE/WEB ADDRESS*. You have to let buyers know how to reach you.

And here is some more information you may want to include:

- *Beds/baths*. I always suggest that you list how many bedrooms and bathrooms your house has. Many buyers are looking for a certain size of house. For example, yours may be a four-bedroom, three-bath house. This is a plus. (If you have only two bedrooms, this is a minus, and you may want to leave this fact off the sign.)
- *Special feature*. You don't really have room for more than one. Typically you might say "Pool" or "Spa" or "Large Yard." Often this can be attached as a separate, smaller part of the sign.
- *SHOWN BY APPOINTMENT*. This is an important part of your sign. Without it, you will have people knocking at your door constantly. You may still have some of these. But, hopefully, most people will call first and you can screen them before admitting them to your home.

Where Do I Put the Sign?

Placement of the sign is important. It should be clearly visible from cars traveling both ways on the street. If necessary, particularly for corner lots, you may need to post separate signs, one at each end of the property. Often, you may want to have two signs placed back-to-back in front of your property.

A sign parallel to the house might be difficult to see except when someone is right in front. A double sign placed perpendicular to the house can be read easily by people in cars as they drive by.

A word of caution: Some cities restrict the kind of sign you may put on your home. Check with your local zoning department. Many condominium associations prohibit owners from putting signs in their front yard. You may be limited, in this case, to a small sign in a window.

Use an Information Box

The sign is an attention getter, but by itself, it isn't going to hook a prospect. It may cause someone to slow down, look at your home, and jot down the phone number. However, they may not have a pen handy or a piece of paper, or the whole thing may seem like too much hassle at the time.

A prospect needs more information than is on the sign to determine if this is a house to be considered. Thus, many good agents have taken to hanging an information box just below the For Sale sign. So should you.

The information box contains copies of a leaflet that gives much more detailed information on the property. It answers some of the potential buyers' questions as well as whets their appetites to see the house. The leaflet is a great marketing tool, and I urge you to create one for yourself.

You can easily build the information box yourself. All you need is a small wood or metal box that will shed water and keep direct sunlight away. (Sunlight will tend to fade whatever's written on your leaflets.) Hang the box on the post holding the sign and label it "For More Information" or "Free Leaflet" or "Free, Take One."

Potential buyers will get the idea. They'll stop the car, get out, and pick up the leaflet. Instantly they have a host of information about your home.

It's a good idea to be careful about what you put in and leave out of the leaflet. Something you leave out may be the very item that will make a buyer really enthusiastic about your property. If this sheet is done properly, it will give all the information a buyer needs to decide that your home is one that she may want to look at further.

Note: Many by-owner websites will send you a printout of the information on your website in the form of a brochure that can be used as a flyer.

Be careful not to include too much information on your flyer. For example, never include confidential financial information, such as your existing mortgages. Don't put down what you originally paid for the property. These sorts of things may come up later, but they shouldn't be the first thing that a potential buyer sees.

Information to Put in Your Info-Box Flyer

Buyer's guide to (address goes here)_____

Price_____

Contact_____

Grammar school_____

Intermediate school_____

High school_____

# of Bedrooms_____

# of Baths_____

Size of garage (1-, 2-, or 3-car)_____

Air conditioned?_____

Pool or spa?_____

Lot size_____

Home's square ft. _____

Age_____

Special features:_____

Photo (color, if possible) of your house

Your phone number/Web address (large) goes here.

KEY CONCEPT *Be sure all information in your advertising is accurate.*

Always include a photo of your house on your flyer. The old adage "a picture is worth a thousand words" applies here. Just being able to see your house often will allow a potential buyer to determine whether or not your place is in the running.

You don't have to be a professional photographer (or hire one) to take the picture. Any point-and-shoot digital camera will do. Try to take the picture on a day that is overcast. The house will come out quite clearly. If you take the shot in bright sunlight, you'll end up with too many shadows.

The information leaflet above won't cost all that much to produce. You can handle the typing yourself and get the sheet reproduced for about a nickel a page at most copy centers. A 4" × 6" color photo is more expensive, but it still can be produced for between $0.25 and $0.50 a flyer if ordered in quantities and attached to each sheet. (Or, a passable digital image can be printed right along with the text, preferably in color.)

Don't Keep It a Secret

Once you've got this leaflet, it would be a shame not to go around and pin it up at a wide variety of other places where potential buyers might stop by. Here are some suggestions.

Housing Offices. Schools, military installations, and larger corporations often operate housing offices for their people to help them find places to live. Often these people are looking to buy. I suggest that you contact anyplace near your home (within a 25-mile radius) and ask the staff if you can hang your leaflet in the office. Most of the time, they will be happy to let you do this. While you can call and then send in the leaflet, my suggestion is that you actually stop by. That way you'll know that it actually gets hung up.

Bulletin Boards. Shopping centers, stores, libraries, civic centers, public buildings, and other areas often have a public bulletin board. Don't be shy about hanging your leaflet. Just keep in mind that you will have to go back every couple of weeks to be sure it's still hanging there. Sometimes it's a good idea to attach a half-dozen small sticky notes to the bottom of your sheet with your address and phone number so that anyone interested can take this information. Otherwise, people tend to rip down the leaflet.

Should I Buy Newspaper Ads?

Free publicity is what we've considered thus far, getting the information out for no cost. (Yes, it will cost you for a sign and a leaflet, but after that, the publicity doesn't cost anything.)

Unfortunately, to reach the largest number of people in a reasonable amount of time, you probably have to go one step better: to paid advertising. This usually takes the form of your local newspaper.

The trouble with newspaper ads is that they are so expensive. If your paper has even a modest circulation, it can easily cost you $25 a week for a tiny ad and much more for an ad in which you can elaborate on your home. Nevertheless, to get the word out, you can't afford to miss this important medium.

My suggestion is that you try both kinds of ads, the little inexpensive ones and the bigger, more descriptive ads. (We'll look at examples of both in just a moment.) You may want to alternate ads on different weeks. One word of caution: Never run the same ad for more than a week. When potential buyers see the same ad run over time, they begin to recognize it and often think of it as that house that still hasn't sold. You don't want readers to think of your house as stale on the market. Hence, my suggestion is that you create a number of different ads and rotate them.

Also, you may find that you have a choice of where to place your ad. In my community, there are one major and two local paid newspapers plus at least three flyers that are delivered free around town. All accept paid advertising. Obviously, I can't advertise in all six, as it would be prohibitively expensive.

Therefore, I suggest that you do what I do, which is to borrow the marketing savvy of those whose business it is to know which papers get the most attention. I get a couple of copies of each and see which ones carry the most real estate advertising, particularly advertising by agents whose livelihood depends on knowing how to get the most out of their advertising dollar. Typically, one or maybe two newspapers or flyers carry a significantly larger number of ads for homes than the others. I use those publications for my own ad and suggest you do likewise. Of course, if after a couple of tries you get poor results, you can always switch to a different paper.

Try Small Ads

The small ad has only the most meager ingredients (see below), and it usually reads as one long sentence and is often heavily abbreviated. The ad itself can vary enormously, but you're simply not going to get a whole lot into just three to five lines.

By the way, many sellers, particularly those old-timers who have done this many times, swear by this small ad. They say that real buyers comb the newspapers and look especially for the tiny ads that include the words "by owner." They claim that these small ads often get twice the response of much larger ads. My own experience tends to confirm this.

Lead with "By Owner." The expression "For Sale by Owner" is one of the biggest selling features. Buyers know that they may have already seen properties advertised by agents (because of their cooperation through listing services). However, if it's by owner, unless they've been by your house, chances are they haven't seen it.

Basics to Cover in an Ad
- *FSBO.* Usually this means the ad starts with the words "By Owner."
- *Price.* Buyers shop by price. If your house is $200,000, you're wasting your time with buyers who are looking for $100,000 or $300,000 homes.
- *Location.* Buyers within a price range always shop location. You needn't give out your street address. Just give the neighborhood or the area of town.
- *Size.* Typically this means the number of bedrooms and bathrooms.
- *Best selling feature.* It could be a large lot or a pool/spa, the fact that the home is redecorated or has an extra room, or some other attribute.
- *Inducements.* This could be words indicating that you are eager to sell or that this is an especially good buy or some other factor that will motivate a buyer to call. *Phone number/Web address.* Forget this and the ad's a waste.

Of course, you may want to switch and stick the most important feature as the lead. It could be the size, the location, the features, anything. Just be sure that somewhere in the ad you also include the fact that you're selling FSBO.

A Short but Effective Ad

BY OWNER
$205,000, split-level, Shadow Hills,
4 + 3, Pool, Large lot, Anxious
555-9087/*www.owners/xxx.com*

Larger Ads

As your ad gets larger (and more expensive), you can afford to expand on the features of what you're selling. However, you want to be sure that you don't waste space (and money). What you say should be the most powerful inducement possible to snag buyers.

To accomplish this, I suggest you limit each ad to a single positive theme; that is, point out one main way in which your house is different, and a better deal, than other homes on the market. You have to identify what makes your home outstanding.

Writing an Ad That Pulls. Large corporations spend billions of dollars annually to come up with catchy advertising that will sell products. Hence, you may think, what chance do you have of writing a winning ad for your home?

Your chances, actually, are excellent. The reason is that you don't need to create an advertising campaign or write a hundred words of great copy. You need only two or three good ads to alternate in the newspaper. Further, you can save a couple of Sunday papers (when the real estate advertising is heavy), note those ads by agents that catch your attention, and base your ad on their wording and format. They say that copying is the sincerest form of flattery, and while I don't suggest you copy someone else's ad, you should be able to borrow the idea without any problem. Another bit of wisdom is that there's nothing new under the sun, which means that the ads you see were probably themselves based on other advertising.

Words That Make Your Home More Salable. Here is some suggested language to put in your ad to excite buyers:

- Good price
- Owner-assisted financing/low down/low payments
- Great location
- Larger size than…
- More room (bigger lot, more bedrooms)
- Unusual features

As noted above, it is important to get across the main theme in your ad. Therefore, I've included a number of ideas, all of which are based on actual ads taken from several newspapers over a period of a few weeks. By the way, you may want to vary the theme of your ad from week to week. If you find that pushing the size of your property doesn't work, you may want to push the low down payment or reduced price. At different times, buyers respond to different incentives (depending on the economy, market conditions, what's available, etc.).

Feature Price. The incentive here is that your price is lower in some way. If you can say that yours is the lowest-priced three-bedroom, two-bath home in your tract, it's a great come-on. Just be sure it's true. A safer tactic can be to advertise your price outright or, as below, emphasize that your price is lower than it was before.

Of course, also keep in mind that while your theme is what may catch a reader's eye, it's all of the other features that will convince that reader to make the call.

Two Sample Price Ads

REDUCED!

For quick sale: Split-level with fireplace, great area close to top schools, manicured lot, recently painted, new carpeting, 4 + 2 with FR.
Make offer and move in before summer's over!
By owner. $289,950,
555-2345/*www.owners/xxx.com*

SELLER DESPERATE!

Must sell, make offer. Top location, four large bedrooms with bonus room over garage. Formal dining room with wet bar in den.
Lender is threatening, see now.
$479,950 by owner.
555-2211/*www.owners/xxx.com*

Feature a Low Down Payment or Better Financing. Here your goal is to attract buyers who don't have enough cash to purchase a house in the normal way. Your advertising must emphasize the financial aspects. The buyer can get in with a lower-than-normal down payment, lower monthly payments, or greater ease in qualifying for a mortgage.

Remember: Always put the theme of your ad into the lead. The first line, or lead, is what catches attention. If it's something that readers want, they will read on with interest. Otherwise, they'll just skim past it. Also, remember that each time you emphasize one aspect of your property or financing, you downplay another. If you point out the wonderfully low down payment, a buyer with enough money to put down but who needs easy qualifying for a mortgage may skip right over it. That's why I suggest running several ads on alternating weeks, each emphasizing a different theme.

Note that when you're advertising the financing, sometimes it isn't necessary to include the exact price. After all, a potential buyer has all the necessary information in this ad if he is looking for easy qualifying (assumability, interest rate, and monthly payment). Often a fully assumable loan at a good interest rate will allow the seller to get a better price, assuming that it's an unusual situation for the market.

Sample Low Down Payment Ad

LOW DOWN PAYMENT!
Only $3,000 moves you in! Seller will carry 15 percent second at
reduced interest rate. Hurry, won't last long. Two-bed adult condo,
$197K by owner.
555-2211/*www.owner/sxxx.com*

Sample Financing Ad

ASSUMABLE LOAN!
FHA fully assumable 6%. Pmts. only $1,337 per month.
Seller will consider financing part of down.
Choice location; must sell by April 1 or lose! Come see,
make offer today.
By owner. 555-2211/*www.owners/xxx.com*

Be careful of advertising something that is commonly available. In some markets, for example, virtually every other inexpensive house used to have an assumable loan, so emphasizing that wouldn't impress too many buyers.

Feature Your Amenities Ad. In some areas and in some markets, it's not price or down payment that sells; it's what the house itself has to offer. This is particularly the case if your home is in a more exclusive area.

Here the owner is emphasizing all the special amenities of this house. Presumably, buyers in this price range are looking for features, rather than terms and price. (This isn't always the case; most of the time, buyers are concerned about price and terms as well. But all things being equal, amenities will sell.)

The ad below was taken from a paper near San Francisco (where prices are among the highest in the country). While the house must be nice, the advertisement actually wastes the owner's money. In this price range and suburb, one would expect hardwood floors, air conditioning, a three-car garage, and good location. Mentioning these features isn't going to impress the reader.

Furthermore, the phrase "must see to appreciate" is frequently found in real estate agent ads and is often used to describe a property that's really in a poor location. Hence, using it here is likely to make potential buyers wary. The ad would do far better to emphasize features truly exclusive to this house.

Sample Features Ad That Doesn't Work

EXECUTIVE MANSION!
Big 5 + 4 with lighted tennis court. Solid wood
throughout, oak floors, air, 2-story, pool with spa, gardenlike setting,
secluded, 3-car garage, choice location, has it all.
Must see to appreciate
$1.9K, By Owner, 555-5551.

The ad below has fewer lines than the one preceding it, yet it has more of the specifics that appeal to the kind of buyer this seller wants to attract. The rule here is, that when in doubt, be as specific as possible.

Sample Features Ad That Does Work

EXECUTIVE MANSION!
Huge 5 + 4 with two-story view of Mt. Diablo, wine cellar, pool/spa,
lighted tennis court, secluded, in-town location, one-of-a-kind.
$1.9K, By Owner, 555-2211/*www.owners/xxx.com*

One point to reemphasize: Don't put the address in the ad. The address not only lets potential buyers know where the house is; it also lets those with robbery on their minds know. Let the buyers call. Screen them on the phone. Then arrange for a time to show the property when you know you'll be there. We'll discuss this more in later chapters.

Feature Size. Sometimes what makes your house special is its size or the size of the lot. If so, you need to get that information to the reader. Once again, however, remember that you may have the biggest house or lot in town, but if the price and terms are wrong, it probably still won't sell. Just having a big yard or home isn't by itself necessarily all that wonderful.

Another Sample Features Ad That Doesn't Work

ROOM TO ROAM

A full 1/3 acre with 11 mature fruit trees. Zoned for horse lover,
includes barn with new roof. Low-maintenance/low-water irrigation
system. Ranch house with in/out gas barbecue, over 2,600 usable ft.
of space. Circular drive and more.
$519,950, FSBO—Call 555-5432.

In an ad taken from a Los Angeles paper, this seller is pointing out that the one-third acre has fruit trees and a barn, in case a horse owner is looking for property. In other words, it isn't just space but is usable space.

The drawback here is that one-third acre is probably too small for horses and fruit trees, and this fact won't be lost on a potential buyer. You can't really advertise that you have room for horses unless you are selling a pasture.

The Unusual Feature Ad. Finally, there's the ad that offers a special feature. It could be an indoor grill, an added-on playroom, a special décor, or, as below, the location of the property.

Unusual Feature Ad

LOCATION, LOCATION, LOCATION!

It's everything, and this home has it all located next to top shopping
and transportation in the heart of the desirable Westlake area.
3 + 2 with wet bar, spa, and RV parking.
$190K by owner. Call 555-1122.

Caution: Many owners feel that their property is well located when, compared with other properties, it isn't. My suggestion is that you ask several agents to name the best feature of your home. They can often point out whether it's really location or something else.

Words That Catch Buyers

When it's time to write your ads, either for a newspaper or for an Internet site, you should be aware that certain words have special appeal while others have negative connotations. The language you use should try to entice the buyer, to make her want to call you to see the house in person. Here are some good words to use:

Instead of this...	...use this.
Looks Good	Charming, Special, Breath-taking views
Feels Good	Comfortable, Roomy, Relaxed
Close In	Handy, Convenient, Fast, Easy Access
Expensive Home	Elegant, Executive, Gracious, Classic, Exclusive
Well-Located	Close to schools, Next to shopping
Large	Spacious, Open, Huge, Roomy
Low-Priced	Starter home, Value-oriented, Affordable
Tiny	Cottage, Cozy, Snug
Made Well	Quality-built, Well-crafted, Lasting
Old	Traditional, Classic, Timeless, Vintage, Historic
Foliage	Tree-lined, Shady, Parklike
Full Features	Fireplace, Spa, Pool, Tennis

My suggestion is that you highlight the most important extras that your home has. For example, perhaps your home's best single feature (after its size, number of beds and baths, and so on) is the fact that it has an oversize patio with gas grill in the back. Your ad might begin "Barbecuer's Delight..." before going on to describe the other features of the home.

Or perhaps you've got a backyard filled with fruit trees. You might begin "Pick Fruit Right Off Your Own Trees...," then go on to describe the rest.

Perhaps the best feature isn't in the home itself but rather that it's in an outstanding school district. You might begin "Education Counts..."

Remember, when describing your home's features, you should not be dull or bland. Rather, this is an opportunity to hook buyers, to grab them by appealing to what may tickle their fancies—what, at a very important level, they want most from your home.

Advertising Elsewhere

A variety of other avenues of advertising may be open to you. A promising new medium is cable television. Most cable systems have a public access channel that is open to a wide variety of local programming.

Often the public access channel will run a commercial for a product, say your house, for a nominal fee to cover setup costs. The fees are typically under $50 and often around $25. You can prepare a short commercial of, for example, 30 seconds using a home camcorder. You can show the front, back, and inside of your home as well as describe the price, terms, and attributes. It's really amazing what you can get into a 30-second slot.

I urge you to try this avenue. Keep in mind that the only people who are likely to watch and listen to this sort of commercial are buyers, but, after all, who are you looking to attract?

Talking Up Your House

Finally, there's the tried-and-true method of talking up your property. How many people do you come in contact with during a day? A week? If you're working and socially active, the number could actually be in the hundreds. My suggestion is that you bring up the subject of your home for sale with everyone you meet. Talk to your coworkers, your neighbors, the lunch counter cook, your friends—everyone and anyone.

You never know who's looking to buy a house. A few of the people to whom you talk, if they aren't in the market themselves, may know others who are. Think of it as starting a rumor. It expands as it goes, reaching more and more people. Eventually it may catch the ear of just the right buyer for your home.

Working the Checklist

The checklist that follows gives you the potential sources for finding prospects for your FSBO. You aren't finished advertising your property until you've got a check in each column. Don't forget the less-formal technique of informing friends, relatives, and coworkers that your house is for sale.

Getting-the-Word-Out Checklist

- ☐ List online
- ☐ Use a flat-fee MLS listing
- ☐ Sign (visible from both directions)
- ☐ Information box
- ☐ Talk it up (to friends, associates, relatives, and so on)
- ☐ Information leaflet (or flyer)
- ☐ Distribute leaflet at
  - ☐ Housing offices
  - ☐ Bulletin boards
  - ☐ Shopping centers
  - ☐ Malls
  - ☐ Schools
- ☐ Short newspaper ads
- ☐ Longer ads

10 Getting Agents to Work for You

MANY PEOPLE SELLING FSBO think of agents as the enemy. Since agents are in it for the commission and since you're trying to avoid paying that commission, you may see the relationship as adversarial.

Nothing could be further from the truth.

The agent can and should be the friend of the FSBO seller. Indeed, very often it is an agent who will find a buyer for your home in the most timely fashion. Remember, your main goal is to sell your home. If working with an agent best accomplishes that, you'd be foolish not to do so.

Do you have to pay a commission?

You'll probably have to pay a *partial* commission. Obviously, no agent is going to work for free. However, if you fulfill the role of the seller's agent, then you only need to pay for the buyer's agent. (Buyer's and seller's agents are technically defined later in this chapter, but for now their meaning is simply that a buyer's agent represents the buyer and a seller's agent the seller.) That's typically half a commission, or less.

In this chapter, we're going to look at four different ways of getting brokers to work for you:

1. Flat-fee MLS
2. Cobrokering with a buyer's agent who drops by with a buyer

3. Working with a fee-for-service broker

4. Listing with a discount broker

The Flat-Fee MLS

Today, you can list your home on the multiple-listing service (MLS) so that most agents (those who are REALTORS® or REALTOR Associates®) can work on it as if it were their own listing. On the MLS, the information on your home is shared by all the agent members. They know all its vital statistics such as price, size, location, and so on.

Why Is It Important to Work with Agents?

Agents have resources that are not available to you as a FSBO seller. These include many more contacts with potential buyers than you're likely to get. Keep in mind that no matter how much effort you pour into selling your home, you're still a part-time seller. (You're working full-time at your regular employment.) The agent, on the other hand, presumably works full-time at selling. It stands to reason that the agent will see a lot more buyers than you will. (It's been estimated that at one time or another, 90 percent of all buyers out there are working with an agent.) Thus, when you list on the MLS, by enlisting virtually all of the agents in your area, you increase your exposure enormously.

KEY CONCEPT *When you list on the MLS, your home is normally also picked up and listed on www.realtor.com, the most-examined real estate website by buyers. Many of these listings are also repeated on sites such as www.yahoo.com and www.aol.com. Since an estimated 75 to 80 percent of home buyers first check the Internet, you're also likely to catch the interest of buyers who are not working with an agent. These buyers may contact you directly. (Unfortunately, MLS listings frequently do not include the seller's phone number, but they do usually include the property address.) Thus, listing on the MLS is like getting a "double pop."*

Listing on the MLS for a Flat Fee

The traditional way of getting on the MLS is to list your home with a full-service agent. You pay a commission of typically around 5 or 6 percent, and the agent lists your property for you.

The new way is the "flat–fee" MLS listing. Here you pay an agent a flat fee, typically around $400, and she lists your home on the MLS.

The listings are essentially the same. What's different is the service. A full-service agent will show your home, do all the paperwork, negotiate for you, and so on. A flat-fee lister will do nothing but list your property on the MLS, and you do the rest of the work yourself.

Does that mean that no agent is involved in the sale and there's no commission? Probably not. Remember, the buyer may have an agent. And that agent will be looking after the buyer's interests (while it's up to you to look after your own). And that buyer will expect you to pay his agent's fee.

Perhaps the easiest way to understand this is to consider the difference between a buyer's agent and a seller's agent. When you list with a full-service agent, she is the seller's agent, the one who works for you and handles the sale. The buyers, on the other hand, are typically represented by their own agent (although, as we'll see later, one agent can do both jobs). Your agent works for you; the buyer's agent works for the buyer. They split the commission, which you typically pay.

When you use a flat-fee MLS agent, you eliminate the role of the seller's agent. But assuming that the buyer is using an agent, you may still be expected to pay for that agent.

Working with a Buyer's Agent

But, you may be saying, why doesn't the buyer pay his own agent? Why should I pay?

There really is no good reason, except tradition. When you list on the MLS, your listing will state what rate of commission you're willing to pay a buyer's agent. Since agents typically split the commission in half, that's usually between 2 and 3 percent (depending on what most agents in the area charge) to the buyer's agent.

Remember, however, that it's money well spent. Most buyers prefer to use an agent, especially when dealing with a FSBO, because they are afraid of making a mistake. They are counting on the agent to protect them. If this is the situation, you are probably dealing with first-time buyers, and there is very little you can, or should, say to dissuade them from using an agent. (If you convince them not to use an agent and later something goes wrong with the deal, they will be very unhappy—read "call a lawyer.")

Should You Agree to Pay the Buyer's Agent?

You have several alternatives. You can refuse to list on the MLS. But as we've seen, that means you're going to miss out on an enormous amount of marketing—not a good move.

Or you can offer to pay the buyer's agent a lower amount. If the going rate for most agents in your area is 6 percent, half of that for a buyer's agent would be 3 percent. You could offer to pay 1 percent, or just 0.5 percent. (That would show those buyer's agents wouldn't it?!)

Again, not a good idea.

Most likely, an agent who's worth her salt won't work as a buyer's agent for less than her full service rate, 3 percent in this case. What with the services they offer, the work they perform, and the liability they incur, that's the only amount a good buyer's agent will accept. Thus, if on your listing you state you'll only pay 1 percent, this agent isn't likely to bring buyers to see your home. Why should she when the house down the street will pay 2-3 percent?

 KEY CONCEPT *Ethically, an agent should show buyers the home best suited to them, regardless of the commission rate. However, in the real world, if you were a buyer's agent, would you show a home that paid a 3 percent commission or one that paid a 1 percent commission?*

What it comes down to is that you can either pay the going rate, or you can figure agents will go elsewhere. And if they go elsewhere, you've defeated a main purpose in listing on the MLS.

What About a Short Rate?

Some FSBO sellers who do a flat-rate MLS listing will in fact offer a short commission—less than half the going full rate. Instead of 3 percent, they offer 2.5 or even 2 percent. It's still a lot of money to the seller, and if your house is perfect for a buyer, these sellers gamble that an agent will show it anyway, regardless of the short commission rate.

With a short rate, the sellers are risking not making a sale. They assume that an ethical agent will still show an interested buyer the home. In that case, they'll save a substantial amount on the commission. (Saving 1 percent on a $350,000 sales price is $3,500—not an insubstantial amount of money.) But who knows what will happen?

Should I Cobroker with an Agent Who Stops by with a Buyer?

Let's put aside the flat-rate MLS listing for a moment and move on to talk about a FSBO seller who has simply stuck a sign in the front yard, perhaps listed *only* on an online by-owner site, and advertised in a local paper. This seller's house is not listed on the MLS.

One day, a broker comes knocking at the door. The agent says that he has a buyer who's very interested in a home just like yours. The broker would like to bring the buyer by to see if he can make a deal. However, before he does so, he wants you to sign a listing, typically good for just one day, so that he can safely show the property without fear you won't pay the commission.

He wants a buyer's broker's commission—say it's 2.5 percent.

Remember, you haven't done a flat-fee MLS listing. You haven't agreed to give half a commission to any agent. But here's a broker, presumably with a buyer. What should you do?

If it were me, I'd sign the listing and let the agent show the house. After all, my goal is to sell as quickly as possible. And if it's a down housing market, a quick sale may mean avoiding the house's sitting unsold for six months, a year, or longer.

What If I Don't Sign?

Then the agent will probably disappear, and you'll not see him or, likely, the buyer. Thus, you can either pay the agent what he wants, or he (and presumably his buyer) will go elsewhere.

But will the buyer really go elsewhere? If the buyer has already driven by the property and is in love with it, the buyer can still come back and purchase directly through you (provided she hasn't signed some sort of exclusivity arrangement with her agent). Or the buyer can go to another agent who is more amenable to taking a lower commission cut. Or the buyer can pay the agent themselves!

If you've got a buyer who's really hooked, rejecting the agent probably will not reject the buyer. Yes, the agent may argue powerfully to the buyer to look for another home. But if the buyer wants your home, then she'll find a way to get to you. But how often do you really think a buyer is so hooked by just driving by?

By the way, even if the agent originally showed the buyer the property, you are under no obligation to pay the agent a commission unless you've signed a listing agreement. This is especially the case if the buyers first found your home on their own and signed in. In theory, they belong to you more than to any agent!

What About Going around the Agent?

What about refusing to pay an agent a commission after the buyer appears and is ready, willing, and able to buy?

If you've signed a flat-fee MLS listing that offers a commission of, say, 3 percent to a buyer's agent, you're bound to pay it. If you sign a one-day listing with an agent for 3 percent, you're similarly bound. In theory, if the document was properly executed, the agent could haul you in to court and very likely win an action against you to collect the commission.

But it should never get that far. My own feeling is that you should never try to go around an agent once you've committed yourself to paying. Besides the fact that it's just not right, it usually doesn't work.

What About Pressuring the Agent to Take Less?

Agents know what they're worth, or at least what they think they're worth. If you drive too hard a bargain, even if the agent agrees, very likely underlying hard feelings will persist throughout the transaction. And if problems arise, they will only be that more difficult to resolve.

If the buyer's agent won't take less than you're willing to pay, you can either give up the deal and the buyer, or you can contact the buyer, explain the problem, and suggest she might want to deal with a different and more reasonable agent. My feeling is you should never pressure an agent to take less than he feels is right. It will come back to haunt you later on in a deal.

 KEY CONCEPT *Yes, you may contact the buyer directly. There's nothing to prevent you from doing that, unless the buyers themselves prefer not to talk with you (not likely). Of course, it may all be moot if the buyers, as noted above, have signed an exclusive buyer's agreement with their agent.*

If you do contact the buyers directly, explain that you're a FSBO seller. Explain how much you're willing to pay an agent (if anything) and see if you can't work something out between yourself and the buyers. Perhaps a fee-for-service agent or a discount broker (discussed shortly) would be a solution.

Discussing the commission in an open and cordial manner often will result in making the deal. The buyers may be impressed with your straightforwardness and honesty. After getting to know you, they may be perfectly happy to do a deal directly with you, with no agent involved. In any event, you'll thus have an opportunity to strike the best commission arrangement for yourself.

 KEY CONCEPT *It's important to understand that if you give a buyer's agent a listing, you are not hiring the agent to do the selling agent's work. There are two sets of jobs—one for the buyer's agent and one for the seller's agent. In this case, you are agreeing to do the selling agent's work. Most buyer's agents will adamantly refuse to do your share of the workload.*

Working with a Buyer's Agent: What Will My Workload Be?

Here's what a selling agent normally does and what you'll need to do, if you agree to pay commission and work with a buyer's agent:

- Handle your end of the negotiations with the buyer (and her agent).
- Handle all disclosures.
- Renegotiate with the buyer (and his agent) if necessary after the disclosures are given and professional inspection report is in.
- Work with the escrow officer and title insurance company.
- Clear the title.
- Prepare the house for the transfer of ownership.
- Close the deal.

What Should I Watch Out for When Signing a Short-Term Listing with a Buyer's Agent?

As noted earlier, an agent who comes by with a buyer will undoubtedly want you to sign a short-term listing agreement. The listing will commit you to paying a commission to the agent, provided he produces a buyer.

The key here is to limit the time for the listing. Many sellers will offer a one-day listing, or perhaps a few days, or as long as a week. Remember, you're not listing your home with a seller's agent. This is a buyer's agent who, presumably, already has a client. All that's needed is for the listing to run long enough for the agent to show your property and convince the buyer (if possible) to make an offer. Why would you want to commit to a long listing in this situation?

The listing agreement should specify the time frame. It should also specify the commission you'll pay, if and when the agent produces a buyer *ready, willing, and able* to make the purchase. And it would be nice if it detailed your duties and those of the agent.

Here's a list of the various types of listings that an agent may want you to sign along with an explanation of the benefits and drawbacks of each.

1. *Exclusive right-to-sell.* With this type of listing, you owe the agent a commission regardless of who sells the property, even if you sell the property entirely by yourself. This agreement usually extends to people who see

the property, if they buy for a set time after the listing expires (often 90 days). It's the usual agreement in a traditional listing. The idea behind it is that if the agent is paying for advertising and devoting time and effort to the sale of your property, she has to be assured that you won't undercut him/her by selling directly to a prospect. You would probably not want to sign this kind of listing with a buyer's agent.

2. *Exclusive agency.* Here, the agreement is that if any agent brings in a buyer, whether it's the agent with whom you listed or any other, you have to pay a commission to the agent. However, if you find a buyer entirely on your own (meaning that buyer never contacts any agent), you don't owe the commission to anyone. The idea here is that your agent is protected from other agents coming in and dealing directly with you but is not protected if you find a buyer by yourself. The agent may insist on this type of listing. If you sign, remember that you can't sell using another agent during the term the listing is in force.

3. *Open agency.* Here, you tell any and all agents who come by that you will give them a commission if they find a buyer. If they don't find a buyer, then there's no commission to pay. This arrangement has specific advantages and can be used at certain times. An "open listing" is basically a nonexclusive listing. Many agents won't consider it, feeling that they might end up spending a lot of time selling a property, only to have it sold out from under them either by you or by another agent. (Note: In this listing, you pay a commission only to the agent who brings in a buyer. The agents are not required to split the commission among themselves, although they may.) This is probably the best listing to give a buyer's agent. It in effect says, "Produce the buyer, and I'll pay."

How Does a Short-Term Listing Work?

You've got your house for sale FSBO. You're invested in a sign, leaflets, information box, advertising, and so forth, and there you sit, waiting for a buyer to come in.

Then, one day, a real estate agent drives up and says that she has a client who might be interested in your home. The client is seeking a home like yours in your price range, and the agent would like to bring the client by. However, she certainly won't bring the client over unless you're willing to pay a commission.

Because your goal is to sell your property, you tell her to go ahead, and you sign an open listing agreement. Basically, this says that if you sell to her buyer, you will pay her a commission. On the other hand, if you sell to someone you find or to someone brought in by another agent, you don't have to pay her anything at all.

You want to sell. Here's a potential buyer. Why not?

As noted earlier, if you're smart, you'll give this agent her open listing. After all, her client might actually fall in love with the property and purchase it from you. (Note: To avoid conflicts over who initially brought whom to see the property, it is vital that you keep a list of prospective buyers that you've produced.)

By the way, with this type of listing, you can't cut the agent out by calling her buyer later on and suggesting that the two of you get together without the agent. A properly drawn open listing agreement is binding on the buyer for a considerable time after the property is shown (even though the listing itself may be for as short a time as a single day).

Be Sure the Prospect Is for Real

Real estate agents know that every FSBO is a potential listing. Although it is unethical for them to do so and the vast majority will not, an unscrupulous agent might call pretending to have a buyer and solicit an open listing from you. The agent may then trot someone through your property who could be a brother-in-law or a friend. (How do you know who the client is?)

The point of this little charade is to get close to you. Once you've given an agent an open listing, for example, and that agent has brought a client by, even if the client does not purchase your home, you might be more inclined to deal with the agent. In short, the ploy could result in the agent's getting a more traditional listing from you down the road.

One way to handle this is to insist on only a short-term listing. You'll pay a half commission to the agent on a one-day open listing (as described above). In other words, the listing is only for the one time the agent shows the property to this very interested client. This says in a most dramatic way that you're not interested in playing games. If the agent does indeed have a legitimate client, she should be willing to cooperate with you on this one buyer and no other. After all, it's the sale that counts.

If the agent is only playing games, a one-day half-commission offer will often make it not worth the time to go through the phony client routine.

What If the Agent Really Is a Lister?

Unfortunately, many FSBO sellers are so pestered by agents that they won't even talk to them, let alone agree to give them an open listing. Some will even hang a small sign on their For Sale sign that says "Principals Only" or "No Agents."

This is a serious mistake because it hurts you. Remember that your goal is to sell the home. The more people working toward that goal, the better. Keeping agents away, in most cases, will only delay the sale of your property.

My suggestion is that you hang a small sign on your property that reads "Will Co-op with Brokers." This tells agents two things. The first is that if they have a client, you will give them at the least an open listing, presumably for a part-commission. (Agents are well aware of this arrangement and, if they come by, will probably be ready to accept it.) Thus, agents won't see you as an adversary but as a possible source of a commission. They will want to work with you.

Second, it puts them on notice that you are serious about handling the sale yourself. *Cooperate* does not mean that you are willing to give them a traditional full listing. In the trade, it means that you will split the deal, including the commission, with them. In other words, you will work as an equal with any agent who has a client.

The house, in effect, is your own listing. You'll be willing to cobroker (cooperate with brokers) on it.

Can I Increase My Price to Cover the Commission?

Bad move.

Many FSBO sellers use a straightforward approach to price when listing their property either for an open/half-commission listing or an exclusive right-to-sell/full-commission listing. They take the price they were asking as a FSBO and then add to it the commission. That becomes their new asking price.

Signs to Show Cooperation with Brokers

"Will Co-Op with Brokers"
"Will Cobroker"

This kind of sign shows that you know what you're doing and can earn the respect of agents. (A sign that tells agents to stay away, on the other hand, often only serves to earn their disdain.)

Further, such a sign puts agents on notice that they're going to get only a half commission from you, not a traditional listing's full commission. Surprisingly, the above message on your sign, in my experience, results in far fewer agents pestering you and far more serious agents stopping by with clients. It may seem like a contrary thing to do, considering your goal is to sell FSBO, but if it works, why not go with it?

While it is true that the agent, who is in the business, gets more potential buyers to see the property and has a better chance, statistically, of locating the right buyer than you do sooner, it's not true that this input can be added in dollars to your sales price. The value of your home is what the market says it is and not a penny more. (See chapter 8.) As many people have dramatically found out, the market value of your property does not depend much on whether you are selling FSBO or listing. It's simply what the market will bear at the time you are selling.

Thus, if you add the cost of the commission to the price you were asking as a FSBO, and you had the house priced correctly to begin with, you will have just priced yourself up and out of the market. Potential buyers simply will not bother. They'll realize that there are other houses available, as good as yours, for less money, and they will buy those houses instead of yours.

The sad truth is that if you list for a half- or a full-listing commission and your house was correctly priced as a FSBO, you'll get less money out of the deal. You simply can't add that commission to the price and still get a sale. What you gain is the sale itself.

Some sellers will offer their home at a lower-than-market price when selling FSBO to get a quicker sale. However, when this does not attract buyers, for one reason or another, they will list and then jump up the price.

The problem here arises when a buyer saw the house as a FSBO at one price but did not want to buy it then for whatever reason. When this buyer later sees it listed and wants to buy, he probably will balk at paying a higher price. This buyer only wants to pay the original FSBO price, even though an agent is now involved.

In a situation like this, you'll almost never get the buyer to pay the higher price, because he will immediately see that *he* is paying the equivalent of a commission. And unless the buyer has been previously sold on paying a buyer's commission, he will not want to pop for it.

So unless you're in a fast-rising real estate market in which the buyer may be willing to pay a premium, you may end up having to compromise by offering the property for sale at or near the FSBO price and still paying a commission, as noted above. In a down or falling market, overpricing is the kiss of death.

The most futile thing to try is to have two prices at the same time, one a FSBO price and the other a listed price with an agent. The buyer who goes through the agent will always find out and will demand the lower price.

Don't Overprice Your Home

Although we've covered it before, it bears repeating. The very worst thing you can do is to list too high. You'll simply increase the time it takes to find a buyer. Instead of a month, it may take three months or six months...or more.

I have seen this happen many times. The FSBO seller adds on the commission and lists the house perhaps 3 to 6 percent above market. But buyers know the market (from having looked at all the similar homes for sale), so they don't choose your home.

Time goes by—a month, two, three. Eventually the seller realizes the mistake and lowers the price to where it should have been to begin with, but by now, the house is a stale item. It's been listed for so long that agents figure there's something wrong with it and don't bring buyers in. Even at a fair price, the house doesn't get the attention it deserves, and, hence, it still doesn't sell.

Often the poor seller must reduce the price to below market to attract attention and get a sale.

Understanding the Difference between a Buyer's Agent and a Seller's Agent

We've bandied these terms about because at an intuitive level, they are quite understandable. A buyer's agent works for the buyer; a seller's agent for the seller.

However, it's useful to understand that in real estate, things are a bit more formal. All agents must declare *in writing* whom they represent. They may either represent the buyer or the seller or, in a strange blending of the rules, both (called a "dual" agent). Whomever the agent declares for, she owes fiduciary obligation. That's powerful.

Further, who pays the commission is irrelevant to whom the agent represents! That's right: you can pay the buyer's agent's commission, and the agent may still owe loyalty not to you but to the buyer.

The Fiduciary Relationship. The easiest way to understand a fiduciary relationship is by an example. Say a buyer's agent overhears you, the seller, saying that although you're asking $250,000 for your home, you'd be willing to take $150,000 for a quick sale.

The agent is *obligated* by her fiduciary relationship to tell the buyer what you said, giving that buyer a big advantage in price negotiations with you.

On the other hand, if the same buyer's agent hears the buyer say that he is willing to pay full price for the home, even though he's making an offer of $50,000 less, that agent is *not obligated* to tell you, the seller.

In short, the buyer's agent must look out for the buyer's interest. And in a similar fashion, the seller's agent must look out for your, the seller's, interest.

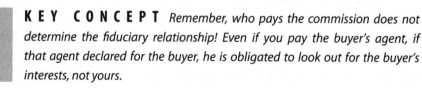

KEY CONCEPT *Remember, who pays the commission does not determine the fiduciary relationship! Even if you pay the buyer's agent, if that agent declared for the buyer, he is obligated to look out for the buyer's interests, not yours.*

From the above discussion, it should be obvious why I think a dual relationship is a poor one to have. No servant can serve two masters equally well, and no agent can serve both buyer and seller equally well. There are times when the interests of buyer and seller conflict, and in such cases, a dual agent is hard pressed to serve both.

Hiring Fee-for-Service Brokers

While you may be prepared to handle most of the chores in selling your house, you may indeed need an agent's expert help with specific tasks, such as filling out the sales agreement or providing disclosures. One way of handling this is to seek out an agent who charges only for the services performed.

What Is Fee-for-Service?

If you take your car in for repairs, there is a schedule of fees, usually prominently displayed, of what it costs to fix various parts. There's one charge for rebuilding a transmission, another for grinding engine valves, and so on.

This is called "fee-for-service." It simply means that you pay for what you use. If the service is repairing the thermostat on the car, you only pay the small charge that's involved. You don't pay a big fee for an engine overhaul, because that's not what you needed and that's not what you got. Why can't real estate fees be the same way?

The Traditional Commission Structure

Historically, agents have only charged full-service fees. The commission rate has covered the broker's handling all necessary services for you.

However, you may not need or want the full services of an agent. You may only want an agent to do a specific service for you. For example, you may only want the agent to write up the sales agreement. Or perhaps help you with disclosures. Or make arrangements for a title search and open escrow. Or any of a dozen other things involved in a real estate transaction. Why should you pay a full commission if you only want limited service?

In the past, as noted, you rarely had a choice. Most agents only operated on a full-commission basis. If you wanted their services, you signed a listing agreement and paid the commission. For that, you got all of their services, whether you wanted or needed all of them or not. Your only alternative was to go FSBO and largely to go it alone.

Enter Fee-for-Service

Today, however, it's a changing world. Real estate is moving into the new century with a new outlook, and many, though certainly not all, agents are responding.

Today there are agents who recognize that you, as a seller, may not want or need full service and you certainly don't want to pay for it. They have responded by offering a schedule of fees for individual services that they perform. Now, just as when you take your car into the garage, you need only pay for the service you select.

A Fee in Addition to the Commission

It's worth noting that while fee-for-service is slowly becoming established, fees added on top of a commission are also coming into vogue. Recently, as competition has increased, meaning fewer sales per agent, some brokers have taken to adding on a "transaction fee" of several hundred dollars. This is *in addition* to the commission.

From the perspective of the real estate agency—maintaining an office, administrative staff, legal consultation, insurance, automobiles, and so on—the commission rates and additional fees must seem justified. However, from the perspective of the consumer, they usually seem just plain onerous and high. This is especially so since much of the work that an agent does (talking up the property, showing clients around, developing leads, and so on) is not really visible—sellers often don't see all the work that an agent does to facilitate a sale. I would resist any attempt to add a fee onto an agreed-upon commission, regardless of how high or low it happens to be.

Where Do I Find a Fee-for-Service Agent?

Your best source is the Internet. Check out websites such as *www.owners.com,* *www.fsbo.com,* and similar sites for leads. How difficult your search is may depend on where you live. In Colorado, for example, there were many such agents a few years ago; then they seemed to disappear. More recently, they are in resurgence. In California, they are harder to find. On the East Coast you can usually find attorneys (discussed shortly) to handle the individual services you need. Usually the more competitive the housing market in an area is (the more agents and the quicker the turnover of houses), the more such agents there will be.

If you use an Internet search engine, be sure to include your locale. You may be thrilled that your first search turns up a dozen fee-for-service agents only to discover they are all located out of state. (Use key words such as *real estate,* *fee-for-service,* and your state or city.)

In addition, agents will generally advertise that they offer fee-for-service. Thus, after the Internet, your next course would be to check local newspapers and the yellow pages of the phone book.

How Do I Evaluate a Fee-for-Service Agent?

You certainly want to be sure that whomever you choose, the person is honest and competent. It would be a horrible mistake to save money hiring a fee-for-service agent only to discover that she made a mistake in the documents or, worse, acted against your best interests.

Qualifying the agent is the same whether he will work fee-for-service or full-service. Here are some things to watch out for:

Does the agent have an office? This may seem simple-minded, but there are agents who work out of their homes or garages. There's nothing wrong with this, except that it usually indicates a certain lack of success that you should find worrisome. If the agent can't even afford an office, just how good is she?

- *Is the "agent" licensed?* In all 50 states, to act as an agent requires passing an exam and obtaining a state license. That doesn't mean, however, that everyone who offers to help you sell your home is, indeed, licensed. Particularly in poorer areas of larger cities, unlicensed people sometimes try to collect fees for real estate services. Any legitimate agent will immediately show you his license.

- *Does the agent belong to a trade organization?* The biggest is the National Association of REALTORS® (NAR). It's a good step in the right direction if your agent can use the designation REALTOR®.

- *Has the agent been in business a long time?* Longevity often indicates good business practices. Quite frankly, it's hard for an unscrupulous, dishonest, or incompetent person to stay in business long. Usually their actions quickly catch up with them (if not the Better Business Bureau and/or the district attorney!). You want an agent who's been in business at least five years. Ask her.

- *Can the agent provide you with references?* Any agent who's been around a while has dealt with hundreds of clients. It should be no problem to provide you with a list (including phone numbers) of a half-dozen recent ones. Call a few. See what they say. Did the agent perform as advertised? Was the work of good quality? Was the client satisfied? Most importantly, would the client use the agent again? This is probably your best indicator.

- *Does the agent have errors and ommissions (E&O) insurance?* You want to be covered in the event the agent makes a mistake, and the easiest way to be covered is with insurance. Agents normally pay thousands of dollars a year for E&O insurance. If they goof and you sue (or threaten to sue), the insurance company moves in and cleans up the mess. (That doesn't mean you'll automatically be paid for a problem—just that if you have a good case, you stand a better chance of collecting.) Ask to see the agent's policy. Be sure it's current and that it's for a million dollars or more. Keep in mind that agents are not usually required to carry such insurance. If an agent doesn't have it and gets you in trouble, he may not personally have the financial wherewithal to handle the consequences. You want an insured agent.

- *Does the agent offer to perform legal services?* An agent is not an attorney, although in most states, an attorney can act as an agent. Agents are not licensed to perform legal services. Beware of any agent who offers to do so. For legal services, contact a professional—a lawyer. (See detailed explanation below.)

What Should I Expect to Pay?

The fees vary enormously with the agent. However, you can expect to pay significantly less in a fee-for-service arrangement than you would for a full-service agent. If you were to use *all* of the services offered, chances are they still wouldn't cost you more than around 1 to 2 percent of the sales price.

Obviously, you can pick and choose the services and fees you want. What's important is that you feel the fees are fair. There should be a relationship to the service performed. For example, you might expect to pay a larger fee for negotiating a sales agreement and for showing your home. You could expect a smaller fee for handling a final walk-though or explaining an inspection report to you.

Overall, however, you don't want to pay more in individual fees than you would end up paying if you simply got a full-service agent. (Or used a discount broker—see the next section.)

Why Would an Agent Offer Fee-for-Service?

That's a good question to ask yourself. If your house is worth $300,000, a full-service commission is about $18,000. Why would a legitimate agent exchange the chance at that big commission for a few thousand dollars in fees?

There are many reasons. Perhaps one of the most common is that the agent hopes to get into your confidence so that, in the event you can't sell your property FSBO, you'll then list full-service with her. In other words, the fee-for-service is a sort of loss leader. Yes, the agent will perform the services, if needed. But the agent's big hope is that you'll sign up for the services when you first start as a FSBO and later, if things don't pan out, you'll come back and list.

There's nothing at all wrong with this, as long as the agent performs as promised. In fact, it's nothing more than a smart marketing ploy on the part of the agent.

On the other hand, maybe the agent is offering fee-for-service because he can't get any listings or make any sales. Perhaps it's a desperation move to stay in business. If that's the case, do you really want the services of this person? (Read again the paragraphs above on evaluating your agent.)

Finally, perhaps the agent truly likes a fee-for-service business. It's clean, and the money is immediate. The agent doesn't have to spend hours and days driving clients around or cozying up to sellers and then get nothing for the time and effort when they don't buy or sell through her. Here the agent performs the service and gets paid. It's neat, quick, and clean, and a good agent can make a good living at it, even at the reduced fees.

When Do You Pay?

Typically you pay when the service is performed. However, if you're going to use a fee-for-service agent, it's a good idea to line the person up well in advance of need. When you have a buyer in hand and need a quick sales agreement is not the time to start looking for an agent. (You certainly won't have time to do a proper evaluation.)

Find the agent early on and establish a relationship. Most agents won't want anything from you. And they'll give you a verbal commitment that when it comes time, they'll be ready to serve you.

Some agents will want you to sign an agreement to work with them and to put up a small retainer, sometimes as little as $100. This locks you in to them. However, I don't really see any advantage to your doing this. Further, if it turns out that you never need the agent's services, you're out the hundred bucks!

What About Using an Attorney Instead of an Agent?

Many people do, and as noted earlier, on the East Coast are many fine real estate attorneys who have long performed in a fee-for-service manner, typically under $1,500 for an entire transaction. However, in the rest of the country, you will be hard-pressed to find an attorney who specializes in real estate. Instead, most are general purpose lawyers who will handle this for you for at regular hourly rates, which can easily be as much as several hundred dollars an hour. Further, since these attorneys don't do this sort of work on a regular basis, you may find they take longer (must look things up) and may not do as good a job as someone who does it day in and day out.

Further, some of the services you may need help with are not all that suited to attorneys. While filling out a sales agreement or creating or reviewing documents may be ideal for an attorney to do, answering buyers' phone calls, showing the home, or providing a For Sale sign are not. In fact, most of the services you're likely to want are best performed by an agent, not an attorney.

Finally, because good agents are involved in real estate transactions on a daily basis, they often know the best way of handling things. There have been many cases in my own experience when I'd prefer the common-sense services of an agent over the legalese an attorney might provide.

Are Agents Legally Authorized to Offer Legal Services?

As suggested earlier, this moves into a gray area that is difficult to answer. In most states, a licensed agent is *not* authorized to provide legal services. For that, you need an attorney. But what is a legal service?

Most certainly it's not providing you with a sign, answering phone calls from prospective buyers, or holding an open house. But what about filling out documents (for example, a sales agreement, the most important document in a transaction)?

In most states today, an agent may not construct a sales agreement from scratch. An attorney must do that. However, most states allow an agent to fill out the blanks in an attorney-prepared sales agreement. In other words, the agent can enter the names of the parties, the address of the property, and the terms of the financing. For the rest, there's usually a series of paragraphs that either the seller or the buyer must check. And usually you are advised to seek legal counsel before doing so.

KEY CONCEPT *Sales agreements today are often a dozen pages long. The "boilerplate" covers the many different situations you and the buyer might find yourself in and provides a way of dealing with them. They lock you and buyer together. These documents are intended to be legally binding on both buyer and seller and should not be entered into lightly. You want a good document that protects your interests. If the sale goes well, you really don't need all that protection. If the sale goes badly, however, you'll need all the protection you can get. Therefore, even if an agent prepares your sales agreement, you would be wise to have an attorney check it over and approve it.*

If that's the case, what do you need the agent for? Can't you can fill in the blanks yourself?

There is the matter of simply getting the form. In California, for example, the sales agreement provided by the California Association of REALTORS® specifies that it must not be filled out by anyone other than an agent. And usually it will only be provided to agents.

Most national real estate companies (Century21, Coldwell Banker, Prudential, and so on) have their own forms, and they will not usually provide them to you. They are strictly for their own agents.

Finally, the forms you typically can find at stationery stores and online often provide only minimal boilerplate language, may need to be expanded to be used effectively in your area, and may not be relevant to the conditions and terms of your deal. You may be taking a real chance by using them.

Thus, when you get a fee-for-service agent filling out a sales agreement, you're not only getting the agent but the agreement as well!

Should You Use a Fee-for-Service Agent?

That's up to you. But keep in mind that only a few years ago, there were virtually no such agents around. You didn't have the option.

Today in many areas you do. And in the future, we may find the fee-for-service agent becoming more the rule than the exception.

Listing with a Discount Seller's Broker

Recently, many brokers have emerged who will work for sellers as a seller's agent for less than the "standard" commission rate (typically 5 to 6 percent). These discount broker are increasingly found across the country, working both independently and as franchisees for national chains.

While negotiating a lower fee has always been possible with any real estate broker, even the most traditional, these discount brokers make it easy. You don't have to negotiate for it. They offer a discounted fee right up front. Even more astonishing, a few offer to provide full service for the discounted fee!

To see how their discount works, we first need to understand the fee structure in general use for agents in real estate.

How Agents Get Their Commissions

When you hire an agent for a 6 percent commission, that particular agent almost never receives the entire 6 percent. Rather, the commission is usually split among several real estate brokers and, possibly, several salespeople. Here's what a typical split would look like:

Typical Commission Split

Total Commission	6%	$12,000 (on a $200,000 sale)
To seller's broker	1.5%	$3,000
To seller's salesperson	1.5%	$3,000
To buyer's broker	1.5%	$3,000
To buyer's salesperson	1.5%	$3,000

Thus, the real estate company (broker) that represents the buyer splits the commission in half with the real estate company (broker) that represents the seller. Then each real estate company (broker) splits what they get with the salespeople who represent buyer and seller.

So the agent who represents you as a seller, if he is only a salesperson and not a full broker, may only get 1.5 percent out of a 6 percent commission ($3,000 from a $12,000 commission).

Of course, there are exceptions to the rule. If the salesperson is very good (sells lots of properties), she can negotiate with the broker for a higher percentage. Top salespeople often get as high as 80 to 90 percent of the half-commission (3 percent) that their brokers get.

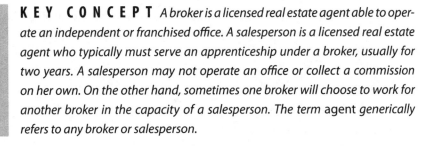

KEY CONCEPT *A broker is a licensed real estate agent able to operate an independent or franchised office. A salesperson is a licensed real estate agent who typically must serve an apprenticeship under a broker, usually for two years. A salesperson may not operate an office or collect a commission on her own. On the other hand, sometimes one broker will choose to work for another broker in the capacity of a salesperson. The term* agent *generically refers to any broker or salesperson.*

How Does a Discount Broker's Commission Work?

As noted, the broker representing the seller typically gets half the commission (3 percent out of 6 percent). A discount broker will accept less than that 3 percent seller's commission.

How much less?

The amount could be either a flat fee or a percentage. Some discount brokers work for as little as $3,000 to $4,000 as a flat fee. (Don't confuse this arrangement with the flat-fee MLS. There, the agent simply puts your property on the MLS and does nothing more. Here, the agent provides some or all of the seller's agent's duties.)

On the other hand, some discount brokers want a percentage. These vary from a low of about 1 percent to a high usually of around 2.5 percent.

Thus, instead of paying the broker who represents you the traditional 3 percent (plus another 3 percent to the buyer's broker), you pay significantly less. The savings to you can be substantial.

Discount Savings On a $200,000 Commission Otherwise at 3 Percent

Discount broker gets...	You save...
1 percent	$4,000
1.5 percent	3,000
2 percent	2,000
2.5 percent	1,000

How Can a Broker Afford to Offer Such a Discount?

In some cases, it's because the discount broker doesn't perform all of the services of a full-service broker. (This is not always the case, as we'll see shortly.)

- Show the property.
- Advertise.
- Promote the property to other agents.
- Field calls from prospects.
- Close the deal.

The discount broker will almost always, however, provide a sign and do the paperwork involved in the transaction (including writing up the purchase agreement). In other words, you are largely on your own when it comes to finding a buyer. But once found, the discount broker will help you complete the transaction.

It's up to you to determine exactly which services will and will not be performed.

Are There Discount Brokers Who Are Full-Service?

There's an old saw about a person who's selling hot dogs on a street corner for 50 cents apiece. A woman comes up and asks, "How can you sell the hot dogs so cheaply? You have to buy the meat, a bun, the condiments. Surely it must cost you much more than two quarters just to buy the ingredients." The salesperson answered, "I make it up on volume!"

An old joke, but what if the hot dog salesperson had a way to obtain the ingredients much more cheaply. Could he make it up on volume? Perhaps so!

This is the position of some national discount brokerages such as Assist2Sell (*www.assist2sell.com*), HelpUSell (*www.helpusell.com*), and others. These usually have franchised or independent offices across the country. They generally offer advertising, call answering, property showing, as well as handling documents and managing escrow. And they often do it all for a substantially reduced fee structure.

Sometimes, as noted, they make it up on volume. Other times, they offer the service by paying their salespeople a flat fee that is typically lower than the commission they might otherwise receive.

Will the Discount Broker Automatically Put My Home on the MLS?

Occasionally they won't automatically list your property on the MLS. The multiple-listing service, you'll recall, is the tool used by brokers to share listings. One broker puts his listing on the MLS, and then all can work on it.

As we've seen, the MLS is without question one of the best and quickest ways of finding a buyer for your home. Remember, today, better than 90 percent of all home buyers at one time or another in the purchase process work with agents. (It doesn't cost the buyers anything since you're paying the commission!) And those agents work the MLS, looking for properties. Thus, if your home is listed there, you immediately have access to as many as 90 percent of the buyers in your area. (There may be thousands of agents working off the MLS in any given area.)

In most cases, discount brokers are also REALTORS® (Members of the National Association of REALTORS®) who operate the MLS throughout the country. Thus, if you request it (and you should!), a discount broker will put your home on the MLS so you can partake of this advantageous service, although she may charge you a separate fee.

However, the discount broker may not want to share his commission on the MLS. Remember, you're only paying a seller's agent's commission here. To take real advantage of the MLS, as noted earlier, you must also be willing to pay a commission to the buyer's agent. As you'll recall, the typical buyer's agent's fee is half, or roughly 2.5–3 percent of a full commission. When you have your discount broker list your home on the MLS, you can specify that amount or anything less.

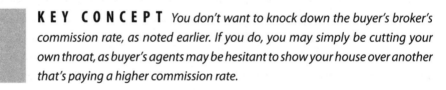

KEY CONCEPT *You don't want to knock down the buyer's broker's commission rate, as noted earlier. If you do, you may simply be cutting your own throat, as buyer's agents may be hesitant to show your house over another that's paying a higher commission rate.*

It's important to remember that in real estate, you're in competition with all the other home sellers. And unless you meet the competition, you'll probably not be successful in selling.

Therefore, my suggestion is that you either try to sell on your own as a FSBO (and just use the limited services of a fee-for-service broker for paperwork, a sign, and whatever else the broker may provide) or bite the bullet and pay the full buyer's broker's commission. That's the best way to accomplish your true goal of selling your home.

How Do I Find a Good Discount Broker?

The rules are pretty much the same as for finding a good full-service agent. You can check with friends and relatives for a reference. Often, hearing that someone had a wonderful experience with a particular agent is the best recommendation you can get.

If you don't know anyone who's has a good contact, then try the tried-and-true methods. Check the yellow pages of the phone book. Check the advertising in the newspaper.

However, for discount brokers, often the best source is the Internet. I've found that most maintain a strong Web presence. They will have a national website as well as local sites that describe the discount services they offer.

What Should I Watch Out for When Selecting a Discount Broker?

There are a number of pitfalls to avoid when selecting a discount broker to work with you. Here are several.

Bait and Switch. Be wary of a discount broker who lures you in with promises of a lower cost, then tries to convert you to a full commission. Once you begin talking with the agent, you may discover that you get few services for the discounted fee. The agent may emphasize that you're unlikely to sell your home using the discount plan, but if you move up to full-service, at full commission, the agent insists you're much more likely to get a sale. If this happens, feel free to walk out. Remember, if you want to pay a full commission, you don't need a discount broker.

Up-front Fees. It doesn't matter if you're paying a reduced commission or a flat fee—the agent should not get paid until your home sells. No sale, no fee/commission to the agent. Beware of discount brokers who want their fee up front. Once paid, they may not deliver even minimal services. The exception is advertising, where you may agree to pay a portion for a reduced fee. However, be sure you control the ads and all your money goes toward them.

Lack of REALTOR® Status. As discussed earlier, to put your home on the MLS, the agent must normally be a REALTOR®. Thus, you'll want to be sure he has this designation. Further, REALTORS® are members of the National Association of REALTORS®, an organization that helps promote professionalism in the field.

Independent Broker or a Franchisee?   There may be some added protections when dealing with a franchise. It may use standardized forms (including a purchase agreement), and it may have policies in place to protect you. A lot depends, of course, on how strictly the local franchisees are overseen by the franchise company. On the other hand, there may be some advantages to dealing with an independent. Here, the broker may more easily be able to design a package to conform to your specific needs. And the independent broker can negotiate freely on services performed and commission fees, without a franchise company dictating specific policy.

A Large Market Presence?   Does the discount broker you're thinking of dealing with regularly run advertisements in the local newspapers? Ads on radio and television? What about a significant Web presence? The more of the market the broker can attract, the more the chances that your discount broker can herself come up with a buyer for your property. Remember, if you've already agreed to pay a buyer's agent's commission, there's no reason the listing discount broker can't pick that up, if she finds a buyer for you, in addition to her seller's agent's fee.

Longevity?   Of course, as with the fee-for-service broker or with any full-service broker, it goes without saying that you should ask how long the discount broker has been in business and if he can provide references. Five years' full-time experience is what I consider a minimum. Any less, and the agent is learning on you.

References?   Ask for references. An active agent should be able to provide you with half a dozen references from property sales over the past six months. (If the agent can't provide you with many recent references, you have to seriously ask why not.) Call the references. Too often, sellers will get a list and be satisfied just to have it. They assume that by being able to provide the list, the agent has satisfied the reference requirement. Not so. Until you call, as far as you know, the list could have been taken right out of the phone book. No, you don't need to call all of the references, but pick three at random. Ask them the usual questions:

- Did the agent successfully sell your home?
- Were there any problems?
- Did the sale go quickly?
- Would you list with the agent again?

Decide whether or not to choose this discount broker based on the answers.

Is the Agent Working with You Full- or Part-Time? Many agents only work part-time. They may be receiving money from a retirement fund, or they may have another part-time job. Part-time agents, may not have the experience you need to conclude a sale successfully, nor may they be fully up to date.

 KEY CONCEPT *In real estate, there are very few wholly owned offices anymore. Most companies, including most of the largest, franchise out their name to individual brokers.*

No Matter What You Choose, Set a Time Limit

I believe the best way of handling these sometimes torturous decisions is to let time do it for you. Begin by deciding to sell FSBO. I believe every seller ought to at least give this a shot.

You can be a purist and do it entirely on your own. Or, if you're like most people and are unsure of handling the paperwork, you can hire a fee-for-service or even a discount broker to do that for you.

Then set a deadline. You'll try FSBO for a month or two months—or however long you decide based on your needs and priorities. And give it your best shot. Using the techniques outlined in this book, make every effort to come up with a buyer.

But if your self-imposed time limit expires and you don't have a buyer, get a full-service agent. Pay the fees. Get it sold.

KEY CONCEPT *Many FSBO sellers waste a lot of time by being stubborn if they are initially unsuccessful in selling their home. They may waste months, sometimes even years, when they could have changed course, listed, and sold through an agent. By doing so, they could have moved on with their lives. Remember, while your goals may be both to sell your home and save on a commission, if it comes down to one or the other, choose to sell.*

11 How to Handle Buyers and Negotiate the Best Deal

I'VE ALWAYS MAINTAINED that the product, in this case the house, either sells itself or it doesn't. Thus, assuming you've fixed and staged your property to show (see chapters 6 and 7), when it comes to selling, your job is largely informational. You need to be sure that the potential prospect is informed of all of the features and advantages of the home.

This doesn't mean that you spend a lot of time talking off the prospect's ear. Often a sale can be lost because the salesperson talks so much that the potential buyer never really gets a chance to see the house and finally leaves rather than listen anymore. What's needed is getting prospects in, letting them look around, and being ready to answer any questions. We'll have more to say about this shortly. First, let's consider just how to deal with prospects at first contact, which usually means the initial phone call or email.

Answering the Buyer's Calls

It's important, vital even, at the outset to understand that when you're selling your home, it's at the buyer's convenience, not yours. I think the analogy of fishing is helpful: when you go fishing, it's not the fish's responsibility to get on your hook;

it's up to you to have that hook in the water, properly baited, and waiting for as long as it takes to get a nibble.

The same holds true for selling your home. It's not the buyer's responsibility to keep calling you repeatedly until finally finding you at home. It's up to you to be sure that every phone call is promptly answered, that information is provided, and that you at least get the caller's name and phone number.

What this means is that as soon as you put your house up for sale by owner with your phone number on your sign, leaflets available, and advertising in the paper, your phone must never be unattended. It's going to take a little extra effort and, perhaps, a couple of bucks, but being sure that the phone is always answered is the first step in hooking a buyer. Ideally, you would be home 24 hours a day, ready to answer any buyer's questions. Obviously, that's not going to happen. So what's next best?

Use Email

These days, one of the easiest and quickest ways to be contacted is through email. When you list online, be sure you give your email address in addition to your phone number. That way, buyers can contact you to make an appointment both to call you on the phone and to come out and see your home.

Use a Cell Phone

Cell phones are inexpensive, and their beauty is that the caller never really knows where he is calling. You could be at home, in a car, out shopping, or almost anywhere. When that prospect calls, you're there to answer.

Using an Answering Machine or Online Answering Service

There are advantages to using an answering machine or service. Some online by-owner sites offer answering capabilities—you can record a message and have private voice mail 24 hours a day.

An answering machine with the proper message can cover for you. Further, you may be more likely to get a call-back number with the answering machine. Here's a typical message you can record on your own answering machine:

You've reached the Smith home. Yes, it's for sale and, yes, we'd love to show it to you. The price is $195,000. We offer excellent seller financing. The house is spacious with four bedrooms and two baths, and the price was recently reduced. Please leave your name and number, and we'll call you back as soon as possible to make an appointment to show it.

I can recite this message easily within 15 seconds, which is the time most answering machines provide for outgoing messages. The message itself is buoyant and informative and has just enough of a hook to get potential buyers to leave their names and phone numbers.

A word of caution: Because one of your goals is to get the caller's name and number, some sellers are inclined to use only an answering machine. That way, they feel they are sure to get that caller's name and number even before they begin a conversation.

Bad move.

Many buyers, sincere buyers, won't leave a name and number. They don't want to be bothered by sellers who may be desperate and make pests of themselves by repeatedly calling back. The answering machine or service is only *second*-best to answering the call yourself. Use it only when you can't be there or if using a cell phone is impractical.

Note that you can use both an answering machine and a cell phone. Use your landline as your basic incoming phone number for ads. Then do one of the following:

- Answer the call yourself from home.
- Use call forwarding to have the call forwarded to your cell phone.
- Use an answering machine.

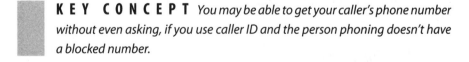

K E Y   C O N C E P T *You may be able to get your caller's phone number without even asking, if you use caller ID and the person phoning doesn't have a blocked number.*

Have a Designated Answerer

The least-desirable alternative, to my way of thinking, is having another family member answer the phone. Sometimes this is inevitable, as when a potential buyer or seller calls in the evening or during dinner and your son or daughter picks up the phone.

Be sure to cue everyone that if a call is about the house, it should go to you immediately. If you're not there, instruct whoever answers the phone to get only the name and number for you to call back. If another person begins giving out information about your house, the person may blow it, presenting the information in such a way that a buyer gets turned off or decides too hastily that this place is not for her.

The worst scenario is a child answering the phone. Even a teenager may turn off the buyer unless he is very comfortable responding to phone messages and knows exactly what to say.

The best situation is having a designated answerer: you, your spouse or partner, or someone else. If a buyer calls and anyone else picks up the phone, the caller should be transferred quickly to that designated person. If the designated answerer isn't home, whoever answered should take a simple message: name and phone number. This method is clear-cut and leaves little room for error.

Have a Dedicated Phone Line

Finally, consider putting in a separate phone line for the time you have your home for sale. This line would be dedicated strictly to calls on the house. All of your advertising (sign, leaflets, etc.) would give that number only. When that dedicated phone line rings, you know that it is someone inquiring about the house.

Yes, a separate line costs a few dollars more, but if you're really sincere about selling your house, it could be well worth the added expense.

Establish Rapport

It's important to understand that when a potential buyer calls, you don't begin the conversation by asking the questions on the phone report below (although a family member who's taking a message when you're not available should ask at least the caller's name and phone number). When you get a phone response to an ad, your sign, your MLS listing, or some other source, you should begin by describing your home.

Describe how it looks, how big it is, how good the location is, and so forth. You should give the potential buyer information. I don't mean that you should just jabber on and on. Listen carefully to what the caller says and try to answer questions honestly and completely.

For the buyers, the first part of the conversation is always a matter of determining whether your house is even remotely close to what they are looking for. Buyers may ask about price, size, special terms, and, most importantly, location. If the conversation goes on for a while and the buyer seems interested, then you can offer to show the house. If the caller agrees, then you are perfectly within your rights to ask for a name, phone number, and other such information. I suggest that the questions be asked informally, as if you're just curious (which you are), not as if you're an inquisitor.

The purpose of the phone report is threefold. First, it gives you a template, a script that you can quickly run through with each potential buyer so that you don't leave out an important question.

Second, it identifies the caller and gives you his phone number plus other information to help you determine if you want to show your home to this person. (When you are selling FSBO, your security must always be a consideration—see the next section.) This is the first step in helping you to qualify a potential buyer. After you've talked for a while, the buyer may provide enough information for you to determine whether he has sufficient income and strong enough credit to purchase your home.

Third, getting the phone number means that you can call the party back at a later date to ask how the house-hunting is coming along and perhaps rekindle interest in your place.

The first seven questions listed in the phone report are pretty straightforward, and most potential buyers won't usually hesitate to answer them. After all, if they're going to come and see your house, they can understand your interest in learning a little bit about them. Questions 8 through 12 are a bit trickier. They are specific questions that will help you determine if this is a real buyer with whom you should spend time or just a prospect.

The Phone Report

1. How did you learn about my house? (Internet, newspaper ad, etc.)
   _____

2. What is your name?_____

3. What is your phone number?_____

4. What is your work phone number in case I can't catch you at home?
   _____

5. Are you a local resident?_____

6. Where do you live? (What part of town)_____

7. Are you an out-of-towner?_____

8. Where are you staying locally?_____

9. Currently own a house?_____

10. Is current house sold?_____

11. Is it listed or FSBO?_____

12. Are you pre-approved for financing?_____

If the caller already owns a house she is living in, hasn't sold it, and hasn't even put it up for sale, you're probably not dealing with a buyer. This person is perhaps months away from being able to buy. You may want to get the number and call back a couple of months later (if your house is still for sale) to see if she is closer to selling the current home.

Keep one thing in mind: because you're a FSBO seller, the caller is going to be just a bit wary of confiding too much in you. After all, you're the person that caller is going to have to negotiate with if he decides to buy. Therefore, don't push too hard. If the caller hesitates and doesn't want to answer, let it go.

If you're done your homework, you will quickly find that you are converting callers to real prospects. People will be coming to see your house. Now it's a matter of dealing with strangers.

The Security Issue

If you're going to sell FSBO, one thing you simply must get used to is showing your home to strangers. Literally hundreds of thousands of FSBO sellers do it all the time.

This is not to say that it is without risk. However, by being observant and cautious, you can go a long way toward protecting yourself.

 K E Y   C O N C E P T *Caution: The suggestions in this section will not eliminate risk to the FSBO seller. There is no way to do that. But they may help minimize that risk.*

Look for an Internet Buyer

When a buyer responds that he saw your listing online, you know that he already has a great deal of information about your property. He's already screened it and thinks it's something he might very well be interested in.

Therefore, you can feel more comfortable in screening this person.

Get a Name, Phone Number, and Address

When discussing the buyer's phone call, above, we looked at a script. However, sometimes a person will call and simply say, "I want to come and see your home. I can be there in ten minutes. Is that okay?"

The tendency is to say, "Sure, come on down."

However, a wiser strategy might be to always ask for name, phone number, and address, no matter how short the conversation. If a person is willing to give an address, even if it happens to be an apartment, even a hotel room, it often means that they are sincere about looking at your home for the purpose of purchasing. After all, how do they know you can't use a reverse phone book or an Internet phone book to check and see if their address is legitimate?

No, this system does not ensure that the caller is a prospective buyer and not a robber, but it helps. And it gives you the chance to call back and confirm your appointment before allowing anyone into your home.

How Should I Set Up Appointments?

When you've got your home for sale, you must make it available when a potential buyer wants to see it, not necessarily when it's convenient for you. If someone calls and wants to see it at four in the afternoon and you had planned on playing bridge this afternoon, cancel bridge and show the house. If a buyer calls at seven in the morning and wants to see the house at eight, if you're convinced she is a serious buyer, show it.

On the other hand, *never show your home after dark*. This is a simple safety precaution. It only stands to reason that if someone has harmful intentions, they will be more inclined to carry them out in the dark when it's harder to see what's going on.

In general, your home must be ready for showing almost anytime, and you must bend over backward to make time for buyers to see the place.

If you think this is a royal pain, you're right. It's inconvenient for you. It's imposing on you. It's downright frustrating. It's also necessary if you want to sell your home. A serious buyer is looking not only at your house but also at many other houses. If your home isn't available to see, that buyer will see another one and possibly buy it instead of yours.

By Appointment Only

My suggestion is that you hang a small sign onto your big FSBO sign (as well as attach a small note to your flyer) that says "Shown by Appointment Only."

This says that potential buyers should call before coming by, which gives you a chance to get names, phone numbers, and addresses. It also gives you a chance to determine if prospects are legitimate and qualified. Of course, it also gives you a few moments to get your house cleaned up (it should, of course, already be in spotless condition!) before the prospect arrives (see below).

Drop-Ins

No matter how much you indicate the house will be shown by appointment only, people will knock on the door and ask to see it right then. Be careful, but try not to turn them down.

Frequently, buyers cruise neighborhoods in which they are interested. They see your sign and think that maybe your house is a possibility. Yes, it's shown by appointment only, but they don't have time to come back, or so they think. So they knock and ask if they can see it now. Chances are that they are serious buyers and you would risk losing a potential sale by not showing your home.

On the other hand, drop-ins are totally unscreened. You don't know anything about them, and you could be putting yourself at risk by letting them in. Below are some suggestions for showing the property at any time. These rules can't guarantee your safety, but they should help.

1. Before letting people in, get them to write down their names, addresses, and phone numbers. Serious buyers shouldn't hesitate to do this. At least confirm this in your phone book.
2. Ask questions such as those on the Phone Report.
3. Never let anyone into your house after dark. It's just too dangerous in the times in which we live. If it's a weekend in the afternoon and lots of people are around and about, you can consider it.
4. *Never show the property when you are alone*, particularly if you are a woman. Simply explain that it is an inconvenient time and offer to set up an appointment.
5. Keep the drapes apart and the shutters and curtains open. This allows people from the outside to see in. No, it doesn't really offer any serious protection, but it may mean that someone with ill intent will think twice, knowing he may be seen.

Does doing all this mean a potential buyer might get away?

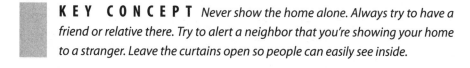

KEY CONCEPT *Never show the home alone. Always try to have a friend or relative there. Try to alert a neighbor that you're showing your home to a stranger. Leave the curtains open so people can easily see inside.*

Yes, it could. But otherwise the risk is simply too great. Think of it this way: if your house were not up for sale, would you let in anyone who knocked on the door? The rules don't change that much when it is FSBO.

Showing the Home

Once you've determined that you have a potential buyer and not just another looker, showing the home is your next task. When you're setting up the appointment, try to leave yourself at least an hour, if possible. The reason is simple. You may have to do some cleaning and other preparation before that potential buyer arrives at your FSBO. Here is a quick guide to getting your home ready to show. You won't have time to do all of these things right before the potential buyer arrives, so plan on doing them every morning or on a regular basis so only a little bit of touch-up is necessary before the showing.

Protect Your Valuables

Never, never leave valuables in the home when you're showing. (That includes inside drawers.) Put them in a safety deposit box, or drop them off with trusted friends or relatives.

The rule is simple: if you don't leave something around that a person can walk off with, it won't get stolen. By the way, this applies whether you're selling by FSBO or with an agent. (Agents can't watch buyers all the time, either.)

When the Potential Buyers Arrive

Greet all buyers warmly and ask friendly questions, such as "Did you have any trouble finding the house?" (if they called on an ad) or "How did you happen to hear of our house?" (This lets you know which of your marketing tools is pulling.)

Another good starting point is to ask if the potential buyers have previously purchased a home from a FSBO. Chances are they haven't, so you can start up a conversation by pointing out that you're selling by owner to get a quick sale. You can note that one of the big benefits to a buyer of your not having to pay a full commission is a lower sales price. (Be sure, of course, that you actually do have a lower sales price.)

Once the buyers get into the house and you've established a rapport with them, think of the biggest rule of showing:

Checklist to Help You Prepare the House for Showing

- ☐ Before the buyer arrives, be sure that your home is neat and clean:
    - ☐ Vacuum carpets.
    - ☐ Sweep hallways.
    - ☐ Wash kitchen and bath floors.
    - ☐ Scrub sinks, toilets, tubs, and showers.
    - ☐ Wash and put away all dirty dishes.
    - ☐ Be sure countertops are clean, neat, and mostly empty.
    - ☐ Put away all loose clothing.
    - ☐ Make all beds.
- ☐ Before the buyer arrives, be sure that you go around and turn on *all* the lights in the house. Even if it's the middle of the day, turn on all the lights. Buyers like homes that are light and airy, so having on lots of lights helps with this. Open all curtains and window shades as well.
- ☐ Before the buyer arrives, check the odors in the house. Bathroom odors will offend most buyers. Use fresheners. Some clever sellers even have a pot boiling on the stove containing aromatic herbs. Or they have cookies baking in the oven, thus giving the house a warm, homey feel.
- ☐ Before the buyer arrives, check the noise level. If there's no disturbing outside or inside noise, you're okay. If there are disturbing noises, such as utility workers out on the street, try tuning the stereo to a calm station. Be careful of playing loud music. It may offend some buyers' tastes. (I don't suggest always turning on the stereo, as some agents do, because having low music on sometimes suggests to buyers that the scene has been artificially set. But if there's noise outside, then even an artificially set scene may be better.)
- ☐ Before the buyer arrives, if it's in winter, light a fire in the fireplace so the house will feel warm and cozy. On an especially cold day, turn up the heat. In summer, be sure the air conditioning (if you have it) is working and lower the temperature. You want the buyer to feel comfortable. (Note: An old trick that car salespeople use is to turn on the car's air conditioning in a test drive. Marketing studies have shown that buyers are far more inclined to move positively when the temperature is just below 70 degrees!)

Should I Try to Close Quickly?

Most of us would like to have the potential buyers walk through, ask a few questions, and then say, "We'll take it!"

It isn't likely to happen that way, at least not on this planet. Very few buyers will walk in, look at your house, and then agree to purchase. The exception here are the buyers who have been looking at a lot of homes, have made up their minds on exactly what they want, and have determined quickly that your house fits their bill. It could happen, but you could grow old and gray waiting for such a deal to drop out of heaven.

What's more likely to happen is that the buyers will spend some time looking at the house and talking with you, then leave. Perhaps a few days later, they will call (or you'll call them) and want to see it again. Buyers may need to see the house several times before actually deciding that they want to buy. That's a far more likely scenario.

Therefore, it's important that you don't try to close on the first showing. The seller who lets the buyers walk through and then says, "Okay, let's draw up the deal," appears naive, puts the buyers on the spot, and could lose the sale. Don't appear to be pressuring the buyers. Doing so would only backfire.

Wait until the buyers call back or until you call them. Then you can ask a few questions to determine if they are really interested.

Should I Hold an Open House?

Real estate agents are always holding open houses. They seem to be a backbone of home sales. If it works for agents, will it work for you? Should you as a FSBO seller hold your own open house?

No, probably not.

First, let's understand what an agent hopes to accomplish with an open house. Numerous studies have shown that seldom does a buyer who comes to an open house actually buy that particular house.

This does not mean that open houses attract only lookers. Quite the contrary, they attract sincere buyers. It's just that they are most frequently not buyers for the house that's open.

Agents hold open houses mainly to find potential clients. Yes, they show the house that's open, but when a buyer doesn't fit, they try to work with that

Biggest rule for showing your house: Get out of the buyers' way!

There's only one rule here, but it's important. It's like the old story about a thirsty horse: "You can lead a horse to water, but you can't make it drink." The same applies to buyers. You can get them into your house, but you can't make them buy. The very worst thing you can do is point out every darling little nook and cranny, every precious thing that you have in your house.

Most buyers hate a pushy salesperson, and when that salesperson is the seller, they doubly hate it. The very best thing you can do, after welcoming them to your house and establishing rapport, is to get out of their way. Yes, you can walk around with them (to be sure they don't take anything), but it's better if you're able to let them wander through your house and see it for themselves. (Remember, you should have removed valuables long before you let a prospect into your home. Remove them from inside drawers as well.)

Wise sellers often go out into the yard or the garage so that the buyers can be by themselves. Your goal is getting the buyers to feel comfortable in your home. They need to have a few moments to feel that they could live in your house and make it their own. They can't possibly do that if you stand next to them the whole time and keep pointing out ways that you've made the house your own.

There are two concerns here. The first, as we've already seen, is security. (You have previously secured all valuables, right?) Leaving buyers alone in the house means that they can, possibly, take something while you're not there to notice. After all, even the most seemingly trustworthy buyers could still turn out to be crooks. You really don't know who these people are.

The second concern is that the buyers will overlook something important. For example, you may have oak floors, an important selling feature, but if the floors are covered with carpet, the buyers may not notice.

continued on next page

Yes, they may ask, but you should be ready to tell them in any case. You can address this situation in two ways. I suggest doing both. When the buyers first come in, hand them a sheet (which you've already prepared) describing all the best features of the house. They can read the sheet as they walk through the house.

Second, when the potential buyers have had some time to walk through and look at the house (you can tell because they start coming out), it's a good idea to pop in and point out all the best features of your home. You may begin with a comment such as "Did you notice that we have all hardwood oak floors under the carpet?" or "Did you see the fireplace in the master bedroom?"

You get the idea. You're simply giving the buyers information on features that they may have missed. Very often, it will turn out that the buyers didn't really see all of the special features of your house, and if they are interested, they may want to go back and look again. Accompany them this time and point out those features.

This is also a good time to begin a conversation about other concerns the potential buyers may have. You can talk about the proximity to schools and shopping. Buyers may want to know about the quality of the local schools as well as about the neighborhood and, in particular, your neighbors.

You can also talk about financing and any special terms you are offering. You may need to help the buyers understand how financing works.

In general, what you want is to be helpful. You want to give the buyers as much accurate information as possible.

One further point: Get time on your side. The longer the potential buyers hang around talking to you, the more they have invested in the house (in terms of time and commitment). If you can get potential buyers to stick around for an hour, you may get yourself a sale. On the other hand, don't give up on buyers just because they quickly walk through and leave. They may have another appointment. However, when you call back later, you may find out that they really did like your house. (We'll talk about the callback shortly.)

buyer to find a house he does want. In other words, for agents, open houses are a major source of picking up clients, buyers and, sometimes, sellers who have to get rid of their existing house before they can purchase.

You, on the other hand, have only one house to sell. If the people coming through don't want to purchase your home, you can't very well interest them in another property or offer to list their existing homes. Thus, in theory, if the vast majority of people who stop won't want to purchase your house, holding an open house is largely a waste of your time.

I said "in theory." In practice, remember that your house is open virtually all the time. Anytime buyers want to see it, all they have to do is call up; give a name, phone number, and address; and you'll show it to them.

Show It to Your Neighbors

On the other hand, it's a good idea to hold at least one open house so that your neighbors have a chance to come by and look at your home. The reason, simply, is that your neighbors may want to buy your home, or they may have a relative or friend who does, or they may be able to suggest someone else who is looking for a place just like yours.

Neighbors can be an important source of prospects. Therefore, I suggest you try at least one open house on a Sunday. Don't advertise it. Just stick an Open House sign in your front yard (readily available in most drug stores). Most likely you'll only get your neighbors. Take the usual security precautions of having several people home, in the daytime, with any valuables locked up. Then welcome everyone (though not necessarily the neighborhood kids, dogs, and cats).

Should I Call Back the Prospect?

Perhaps the most important call you'll make when selling your property is the callback. Some buyers came out; gave you their names, address, and phone number; looked at your house; and left. If you don't call them back, you may never see them again. Also, you may lose a deal that could have been made.

I can't think of the number of times I've called back potential buyers only to have them tell me, "Yes, we were thinking about your house, it's really nice, we like it, and probably would make an offer on it. But we just never got around to calling you."

Don't wait for buyers to call you. Almost all buyers suffer from a kind of forgetfulness that sets in as soon as they see your property. I suspect that it comes about because they feel if they call you back, you'll think that they surely want it, will pay full price, will give you cash, and will meet all your other terms. They may simply be afraid to call you for fear of giving you the wrong impression. (Translate that to mean "a strong bargaining position.")

I can recall talking to buyers who were actually mad at agents (in this case) who didn't call them back when they were really interested in the house. "That so-and-so agent dropped me. What kind of irresponsible action is that?"

I sometimes remind such people that a phone line works both ways: if they were really interested, they could have called the agent or the seller directly. But, somehow, they just never do.

The point is, don't wait around for potential buyers to call you. After a day or two, call back. It could make you a deal.

What Should I Say on the Callback?

Obviously, you will introduce yourself, mention the house they saw, and then ask something like "Did you have any further thoughts on the house?" or "Was there something more about the house you'd like to see?" (thereby offering to show it again).

If the potential buyer reacts by saying, yes, she really did like the house and would like to see it again or, miracle of miracles, "Yes, I'd like to talk about a deal with you," you're on your way.

More than likely, however, the buyer will be restrained and noncommittal and try to get off the phone as quickly as possible. If that's the case, you probably have a looker and not a buyer (at least not for your house). However, don't give up. Just because you don't get a yes right off the bat doesn't mean that you're getting a no.

Always Ask, "What's Wrong?"

After a bit of small talk, ask what's wrong with your house. This is not to say that there is anything wrong with the place. What you should try to determine, however, is what the buyers see as a problem. In other words, find out the buyers' main objection to your property. You might ask a question such as "What about the property doesn't appeal to you?" or "Is there something about the house that you don't like?"

The Basics of Direct Negotiation

Although many by-owner sellers feel perfectly comfortable negotiating directly with a buyer, many find it unsettling. What if the buyer runs down the house? What if the buyer is overly assertive? What if the buyer demands a price lower than you're willing to concede? What if the buyer wants to know how you plan to handle the details of the sale, such as the sales agreement, disclosures, inspections, and so on?

How Do I Establish a Working Relationship with the Buyer?

As the seller of a home dealing directly with a buyer, it's important to see things from the buyer's perspective. And as far as the buyer is concerned, you are automatically suspect.

The buyer suspects that you will do anything and everything to sell that home, including lying and cheating. The buyer sees you as the adversary. Therefore, if you're going to deal effectively with that buyer and come to acceptable terms in a successful sale, you have to establish trust.

How do you do that?

The way to win trust is to be trustworthy. It sounds simple, yet sometimes it can get complicated. As noted earlier in chapter 2, here are the rules to win the trust of the buyer:

- Never personally offend the buyer.
- Never hide a defect in your property.

- Never lie about anything involving the sale.
- Never offer to do something you can't do.

In short, always be courteous, reasonable, and truthful. If you are, the buyer will soon see that you are someone whom she can work with and count on. If you don't, you'll find that distrust sours every buyer with whom you deal. Remember, if you try to hide something or lie, little inconsistencies will do you in. Buyers, who are naturally suspicious, are looking for those inconsistencies. Honesty is the key to establishing a relationship with the buyer. The buyer doesn't have to like you (although that does help), but must respect you if the two of you are to conclude a successful real estate sale.

The potential buyers, if they are even remotely interested in the property, should now explain to you why they aren't willing to buy it. The reasons they give could be anything, but here are some of the more common ones:

- Not the right location
- Too big/small; not enough/too many bedrooms
- Too expensive/poor terms
- Poor condition
- Lacks features (air conditioning, central heating, new carpeting, big yard, etc.)

If you can get a single, good reason that they don't want to buy the house, chances are that you've got real buyers on your hands. Now all you have to do is turn that negative into a positive, and you've got a sale.

Turning a Negative into a Positive

Usually you can. For example, if the problem is price or terms, you can agree to negotiate. This should heat up the buyer's enthusiasm and should result in both of you getting together to discuss things further.

On the other hand, if the house is in the wrong location, there's very little you can say or do. You can point out, for example, "For the location, the price is very good. If you want a better location, you'll have to pay a lot more. Is that the kind of money you were looking to spend?"

If the buyers don't have enough money to move to a better location, then you're dealing with the champagne tastes and beer pocketbook mentality. Your job is to convince the buyers of the reality of the real estate market. Ask them if they've looked around at other houses. (You should have already done this yourself when you established the price.) Explain that for what they want to spend, they simply won't be able to do better than your house. In short, try to bring them down to reality.

On the other hand, if it turns out that they can spend more money for a better area, you can point out that they can also spend less. Why spend more when they could have all the features of your house for less money?

You won't overcome every potential buyer's objections with this strategy, but it's worth a shot. Be creative. As long as you're still talking, you've still got a potential deal. My suggestion is that no matter how negative the answers may seem, try to use the techniques below for dealing with potential buyers' objections:

- Turn a negative into a positive.
- Try to get them to come and see the house again.
- Don't give up.

If the buyers simply aren't interested, don't want to talk anymore, and say "Good-bye!" well, it's just one that got away, and just for today. My suggestion is to put their names on a back page and call again in two or three weeks. Maybe they will have seen more of the market and rethought their priorities.

Yes, you may make a bit of a pest out of yourself. But if you're polite, charming, and even, if possible, witty, they'll overlook that. After all, many sales are made simply because the seller is persistent.

Create a Visitor Book

Finally, ask everyone who comes to see your house to sign a visitor book if he might even remotely be perceived as a serious buyer. If you ask visitors to do this just as they come into the house, most people will be happy to oblige as a courtesy.

The visitor book should provide space for the minimal information: name, address, and phone number. You can also solicit written comments. Some sellers ask visitors to indicate the kind of property they are looking for (number of bedrooms and bathrooms, location, price, etc.) as a way of determining who are the more likely buyers.

There are two purposes for having visitors sign the book. The first is to provide you with a means of calling them back later on. (See the phone callback discussion above.)

The second is to provide the name and address of every buyer who came by in the event that you later list the property. You can specify in the listing, even in an exclusive-right-to-sell listing, that if anyone to whom you showed the house *before the listing term* buys it, you don't have to pay a commission. Your visitor book is the proof of who was there and who wasn't.

Don't underestimate the value of the visitor book. It can lead you back to a looker who becomes a buyer. It can save you a commission. A FSBO seller who doesn't have a visitor book is overlooking an enormous resource.

Note: Any book or even a sheet of paper will do. However, if you go to the stationery store, you can pick up ready-made visitor books. Usually they are designed for receptions or weddings, but they can easily fill the need here. Just be sure that at the top of each page you clearly print (or type) the information you want visitors to record. (See the example of a visitor's book given at the end of this chapter.)

When You Get a Real Live Buyer

One of these days, perhaps sooner than you imagined, you will find a buyer who says, "Yes, I want to purchase your home." You will haggle over the price, the terms, perhaps even the light fixture in the dining room, but ultimately, the buyer will want to purchase and you'll sag back with a sigh of relief, telling yourself, "At last, it's over!"

Typical Visitor Book

Our Address: 2341 Maple Street

Our Phone: 555-4352

Thanks for looking at our For Sale By Owner home. So that we have a record of those people who stop by, please list the following information:

Name _____

Phone Number _____

Address _____

City, State, ZIP _____

Comments _____

_____

Name _____

Phone Number _____

Address _____

City, State, ZIP _____

Comments _____

_____

Name _____

Phone Number _____

Address _____

City, State, ZIP _____

Comments _____

_____

Name _____

Phone Number _____

Address _____

City, State, ZIP _____

Comments _____

_____

12 What You Need to Disclose When You Sell

A MODERN HOME sale often has two rounds of negotiations. The first is when you and a buyer agree on a sales price and terms. You set these out in a sales agreement that you both sign, thus making the deal.

The second round may come about after you have given the buyer disclosures about any defects your home may have and the buyer's inspection report has been completed. Depending on what's been uncovered, at that time, you and the buyer may need to sit down again and renegotiate the price and terms of the purchase.

This double negotiation can be confusing for many new by-owner sellers. Most people tend to think of the deal as having been sealed in stone when the purchase contract is signed. However, as we'll see, that's not strictly true.

The original sale is typically contingent on the house being in pristine condition. Once it's true condition is revealed (by means of your disclosures and the inspection report), a price for a less-than-pristine property may need to be negotiated. Yes, the buyer consents to make the purchase with the sales agreement, but only after accepting the true condition of your property.

Remember, in most cases, the buyer signs the sales agreement under the assumption that the home is in perfect condition. However, if it turns out that there are defects, then the home is obviously not worth as much as agreed when that assumption was made. As a result, the seller must either rectify those defects and bring the home up to perfect condition or cut the price in some way.

It's Like Selling a Car

Think of this way. You've got an old clunker of a car that you want to sell. You advertise it for sale at $5,500.

After a few days, a buyer comes by, drives the car, and likes it. The buyer says, "I'll give you a flat $5,000 for car. But I want my mechanic to check it out first."

You only expected to get $4,000, so the $5,000 offer is great and you agree. The first negotiation is complete. Now you give the car to the buyer, who takes it to her mechanic.

Three hours later she's back. She says, "My mechanic says the transmission is shot and it needs four new tires. The tranny will cost $800 to fix, and the four tires will cost another $400. I'll still take the car but only if you reduce your price by $1,200 and sell it to me for $3,800."

You think about it a minute. The transmission has indeed been making strange noises and has been slipping on hills. And you've noticed those tires are looking bald. But you want your minimum price. So you say, "Okay. You've got a point. But, I think you could get the tires and transmission for less. I'll cut my price by $1,000 and sell it to you for an even $4,000."

The buyer thinks a minute, then says, "Agreed!" The second negotiation is completed.

Consider what just happened. The original offer was made and accepted without the buyer being informed as to the true condition of your car. Once the buyer was informed as to the true condition, the second offer was made and negotiated.

This is the way it's often done when selling used cars. And it's similar to what we've been discussing when selling your existing home. You originally negotiate with a buyer who's uninformed about the condition of your property but assumes it's perfect. Once the buyer is informed about the condition, if there are any defects, the second negotiation occurs.

As we've noted, the condition of your property is usually determined in two ways, by what you disclose to the buyer and by what a buyer's professional inspection reveals. What the latter turns up results in the second round of negotiation, which determines the final price and terms of the sale.

Obviously, the second round of negotiation is almost as critical as the first, as it determines the final price and terms of the sale. Indeed, it's so critical that savvy by-owner sellers will go out of their way to determine what, if any, defects their property may have before putting it up for sale. That way they can hope to eliminate, or at least reduce, the negotiations in the second round. They hope to get a firm price and terms on the first round.

Must You Disclose?

Most states insist that the seller has a duty to inform buyers of any known (and sometimes even unknown!) defects in the property. Such laws came about because too many complaints were heard from buyers who bought thinking a property was in good shape, only to discover later it had defects costing tens of thousands of dollars to correct.

Today, if you don't disclose problems with the property when you sell, it's possible, even likely, that the buyers could come back later and claim to have been deceived. They could even sue for damages and, conceivably, for rescission (which means that you would have to take back the house and give back the buyer's money). While these dire consequences are unlikely, they have happened.

As a result of disclosure concerns, most states have instituted compulsory disclosure laws. Sellers in those states must disclose defects upon sale. Even if your state still doesn't require disclosure, chances are that buyers will insert a demand for them into the sales agreement. Thus, one way or another, you'll probably have to give the buyer disclosures.

The federal government also has lead disclosure laws.

Irwin's Theory of Disclosure

The way I see it, disclosure actually protects the seller more than the buyer. If you disclose a defect and the buyer moves ahead with the purchase, knowing that the defect exists, you're in a much better position. Perhaps an example will help.

I recently sold a property "as is" (meaning I noted defects but did not correct them) where there were significant cracks in the concrete slab foundation. It had not affected the livability of the home, but I wanted the buyer to be aware that a problem existed.

In some parts of the country, a house is built atop a slab of concrete that is poured on top of the ground; there is no basement or crawl area whatsoever underneath. When slabs crack, those cracks are often reflected in cracks in the walls and ceilings as well. Usually rebars (reinforcement steel bars) in the concrete hold the slab in position even if it cracks, but if the problem becomes very severe, the floor conceivably could split, making one spot higher than another.

Usually it's just an annoying problem. But a buyer who purchased a home unaware such a defect existed could be angry enough to seek redress.

Therefore, I gave the buyer a disclosure statement (see the statement at the end of this book) on which I noted that there were cracks in the slab. Expansive soil underneath was unstable, and particularly in wet weather it could cause additional cracking in the house. I also noted there were cracks in the walls and in the ceilings. In short, I gave the buyer every notice possible of the defect. Further, I suggested that the buyer should hire his own inspector to come in and check out the problems, which he did. The inspector noted the cracks as well but indicated they were old and unlikely to cause further trouble.

The house was sold and everything seemed fine, until later that winter when the area had an abnormally large amount of rain. The ground beneath the slab became soaked and expanded, as can be the case with clay soils. The old cracks enlarged, and a few new ones appeared in the ceilings and walls. The furious buyer called, wanting me to fix all the problems.

I tried to calm him down. Then I reminded him that I had informed him of the cracks in the slab, the problem with the soil underneath, and the cracks in walls and ceilings. He said he didn't care. He just wanted me to make repairs, and if I didn't, he would hire an attorney.

I told him that an attorney was a good idea and to ask one what his chances of recovery were. We ended the conversation on that note. It's been several years, and I haven't heard from that buyer since.

The moral here is that I believe it's best to disclose everything. I have become known among associates as one who provides very extensive disclosure statements. My disclosures are highly detailed.

And why not? Most sellers erroneously fear that disclosing defects will cause the buyer to shy away. I have found that not to be the case. Most buyers who are sincerely interested in the property will accept defects, will negotiate the price to compensate for them, or will work with the seller to correct them. More to the point, the property is what it is. If it has a defect, it's better that you get it out in the open than for the buyer to discover it a few months later.

If you want to be extra careful, you can insist the buyer accept the house with the defect "as is," as noted. However, remember that selling "as is" does not relieve you of the responsibility to disclose defects.

How Can I Disclose Defects I Don't Know About?

Changes in disclosure requirements have an added twist that would be comical if it weren't so serious. As a seller, you may be required to disclose defects in your home that even you don't know about!

For example, you could have a bad gas line leading to your hot water heater. You may not know about it, but if you fail to disclose it and, after a sale, there is a gas explosion in the property, you might be held responsible.

Incredible? The theory here is that as a seller, it is up to you to investigate and discover many problems, certainly those involving health and safety, that involve your property and correct them as well as reveal them to the buyer.

As a result, to protect themselves, some sellers hire a professional inspector to look over the property before the sale to determine if there are hidden problems. Presumably, if the inspector gives you a clean bill of health, you're okay.

KEY CONCEPT *Inspectors can't report on what they can't see. Hence, most inspection reports apply only to accessible areas. This often does not include under carpets, within walls, or in other areas the inspector can't reach. Further, to protect themselves against complaints, many inspectors today include their own disclaimer statement in their reports, saying they are not responsible for anything they don't find and, in some cases, even for things they overlooked or misinterpreted!*

Of course, this means that it's to your advantage to have an inspector check over your house. If anything happens later on, you can always point to the inspection report and say that you made a good effort to determine any problems.

However, unless you suspect problems, it probably doesn't pay to hire an inspector yourself. Agents have worked hard to convince buyers that they need the inspection to uncover hidden defects that you, the seller, haven't disclosed. Therefore, most buyers are already primed to pay for an inspection. All you have to do is recommend it, and nine out of ten buyers are ready to pay for it. In reality they are paying, in part, to relieve you of potential liability.

We'll look at inspections in more detail at the end of this chapter.

What Form Do Disclosures Take?

Remember, an inspection is conducted by a professional, who normally produces a written report. Disclosures, on the other hand, are a document that you yourself prepare and give to a buyer.

The simplest method of disclosure is simply to tell buyers about problems as you show them the property. As you walk by the fireplace, for example, you note that it has a crack in the flue. The estimated cost of repair is $1,500. You're prepared to take that off the price.

You have to be careful, however, to document the disclosure—to leave a paper trail. Yes, you may have fully explained the problem to the buyers, but six months later, when they claim you never told them, what do you have to back it up? If you have a disclosure statement describing the problem with their signatures on it, you're in much better shape.

 K E Y   C O N C E P T *Give all disclosures in writing and get a dated and signed acceptance from the buyers.*

The actual form of the disclosure statement will vary from area to area. In some parts of the country, no official disclosure statement exists, and you will want to have your attorney draw it up for you. (As noted, at the end of this book is an example of a typical disclosure statement.)

When Should I Present My Disclosures?

Should you disclose all defects to the buyer up front, or should you wait and disclose them after the buyer has signed a purchase agreement?

In California, which has some of the toughest disclosure laws in the country, a seller may give the buyer a written disclosure statement after the deal has been signed. However, the buyer then has three full days to rescind the deal by refusing to approve the disclosures with no penalty (no loss of deposit) for any reason.

In purchasing property, some shrewd buyers have taken advantage of this California state law to make deals and then continue shopping around, knowing they have a full three days to back out without penalty. As a consequence, wise sellers sometimes give the disclosure statement to the buyer as soon as the deal is made, sometimes even before a deal has been agreed upon!

Regardless of when you disclose, you want the buyer to sign and date an acknowledgment of having received the statement.

What Should I Disclose?

While you can't determine what a professional inspection will reveal, as we'll see shortly, you do have complete control over what you put in (or leave out) of your disclosures. *What* you tell your buyer is wrong with your property, and *when* you tell her, will help determine how both rounds of negotiations turn out.

Obviously, the more defects you tell the buyer about, the lower the price will be. Hence, many sellers tend to gloss over some problems, hoping the buyer won't find out about them. Most sellers fear that when it comes time to deal with disclosures, if they let the buyers know that things that are wrong with their property, they'll lose the deal at worst or have to lower their price at best.

Don't worry. Things usually work out. No, you may not get your full price, but then again, if your home has a serious defect, your full price may have been unrealistic.

Remember, disclosures actually can be the seller's friend. They can help protect you from the buyers' coming back after the deal and demanding that you correct some deficiency in the property. If that happens, you can hold up the disclosures and say, "I told you all about it, yet you bought the property anyway! You have no gripe coming now."

Obviously, it's impossible for me to know specifically what you should disclose about your property. However, a number of red-flag items are of particular concern to buyers these days. Here are the top seven.

Black Mold. Black mold is a kind of fungus that attacks wood, furniture, clothing, carpeting, and most other things left in a wet environment, and it has probably been around forever. The spores seem to be ubiquitous. That means that if you have a wet wall from a leaky pipe in a utility room, chances that over time, black mold will develop. It will probably develop in most other wet areas as well.

Until fairly recently, black mold was considered nothing more than a nuisance. The affected areas were removed and replaced. For example, the leaky pipe was fixed, then the sheetrock with black mold on it might be taken off and new sheetrock put on, taped, textured, painted...and that was the end of it.

However, a series of high-profile lawsuits against insurance companies that refused to pay for more extensive cleanup of black mold has changed all that. Claiming that black mold actually causes serious illness and possibly even death, plaintiffs demanded whole-house cleanups. As a result, insurers have now become very wary of black mold claims. Indeed, most insurance companies have changed their policies to limit their liability when it is found in the home.

After seeing stories of men in bubble suits attempting to fix the problem in infected homes, and even cases where the home apparently had to be destroyed to get rid of the mold, buyers are likewise sensitive to it. In short, most buyers don't want to touch a home that has black mold problem.

Therefore, if you're aware of black mold in your home, it's important to realize that you've got a serious and potentially expensive problem. Most professional pest inspectors do check for black mold in bathrooms, kitchens, utility rooms, and other areas where moisture is likely to occur, so if it exists, it's likely to be found.

In my own properties, when I discover black mold, I quickly take steps to professionally remove it and the moisture causing it. That way, I don't have to disclose that I know of a black mold problem *currently* in the home. However, if the problem was corrected recently—within, for example, the past five or so years—I mention that I found it and describe how it was corrected.

Failure to disclose that you know of existing black mold in your home, because of buyers' sensitivity to it, can result in serious claims for damage repair after the sale.

Keep in mind, however, that whether or not you disclose black mold in your home, if a professional inspection uncovers it, you can expect the buyers to negotiate for a complete cleanup at the least. Some buyers will simply walk away from the deal. And some insurers will refuse to issue homeowner policies.

Water Damage. This can arise from a wide variety of sources. For example, you could have a leaky pipe in a wall. Or your basement could flood during rains. Or your roof could leak into your attic. Or a toilet might not be set properly and could leak. And on and on.

The concern today with water damage is that it can lead to black mold, noted above. Therefore, buyers are very careful to look for any reports of it in your disclosures.

When I have water damage in the home, I take great pains to see that it is corrected. For example, drains and even a sump pump can get water out of a basement. Repairing a roof should take care of it in the attic. Getting the toilet seated properly will help correct for leaks around it. And so on. I also see to it that any damage caused by the water is professionally repaired; for example, wet board, sheetrock, and other materials are removed and replaced, helping to ensure there's no breeding ground for black mold.

Again, if the damage is fairly recent, I will report that the home had water damage and describe how it was corrected. Keep in mind, of course, that just the reporting of it could deter some buyers and some insurers.

Leaking Roof. The assumption by buyers is that the roof does not leak. If it does leak, they will assume you'll fix it.

Even if you sell a home "as is," you should disclose a leaking roof. You just may not be required to fix it.

If a roof in my home leaks, I'll call in a roofer to repair it. Then, in my disclosures, I'll note that it leaked in the past and explain how it was fixed and, finally, that it does not leak now. (Keep in mind the problems related to water damage noted above.)

The advantage of fixing a roof prior to selling your home is that if the buyers learn it's still leaking, they may demand a brand-new roof. However, if the current roof is sound (doesn't leak), they are less inclined to make such a demand.

Power Lines. Some homes are built near high-voltage power lines. If you're right underneath these lines, you can sometimes even hear a distinct humming noise coming from them.

Are high-voltage power lines a health hazard? I don't think anyone knows for sure. Studies done several years ago, which I saw, didn't find any particular problems associated with them. However, other studies could always turn up something new.

Nevertheless, a buyer who bought a home not realizing it was underneath or near a high-voltage power line could become quite unhappy. This buyer could claim that the house was sold under false pretenses and demand compensation or even that you take it back. (It's hard to imagine a buyer not noticing a high-voltage line overhead, but some people just don't look up!)

Therefore, it's probably wiser to disclose the high-voltage lines if they are nearby. How close is "nearby"? It's hard to say. I would guess anything within a quarter to half a mile. But others might feel the range could be farther, or shorter.

Death or Serious Disease in the Home. This is a strange one, but a number of high-profile cases have made it important. Some buyers claim to have been adversely affected, emotionally or physically, when after buying a home, they learned that a previous occupant had died there or had a serious illness, such as tuberculosis or AIDS. Again, the big danger to the seller is that the buyers will come back after the sale and demand damages or rescission of the deal (demand you take back the house).

Therefore, even though it may adversely affect the sale, you might be wiser to disclose any death (particularly if it were murder) or serious illness that occurred on the property.

Damage to the Structure or Foundation. This almost goes without saying. If you're aware of a problem here, you're probably also aware that it will almost surely result in a lower price for your home. Failing to disclose it in the hopes of getting a higher price is likely to lead only to trouble.

Lead Based Paint And Other Toxics. The federal government now requires home sellers (and landlords) to provide information to buyers (and tenants) regarding their knowledge of lead paint in homes built prior to 1978. You must give the buyer/tenant an EPA approved, filled out, and signed form, as well as a pamphlet describing the lead paint hazard. Other disclosures regarding toxic substances such as asbestos or formaldehyde may be required in the future. For the form and pamphlet, check out: *http://www.hud.gov/offices/lead/enforcement/disclosure.cfm.*

What About a Home Inspection?

Now let's get back to those professional inspections. Inspections help inform the buyer of any possible defects in the property. A variety of inspections are typically performed these days. They include the following:

- Professional whole-house
- Termite and pest (required by most lenders)
- Roof
- Soils
- Structural
- Pool and spa
- Any other area of concern

From a buyer's perspective, a professional whole-house inspection is valuable because it avoids the problem of buying a "pig in a poke." Beyond any disclosures you may offer, the buyer hopes to learn exactly what the condition of the property is. If something untoward is discovered, then typically the buyer will want an additional inspection of roof, soils, structure, or whatever. (A termite inspection is handled separately by a licensed pest inspector and is usually a condition of getting financing.)

From a seller's perspective, as we've seen, an inspection can also be helpful. If the buyer orders the inspection, it tends to put the seller in a more solid position. Later on, the buyer can't as easily come back and claim to have bought a defective home. The seller can say, "I opened my home to you. You hired your own professional inspector. If he couldn't find the problem, how could I have been expected to know about it?"

 KEY CONCEPT *A home inspection does not relieve the seller of disclosing any known defects. Rather, it usually helps to uncover defects unknown to the seller.*

On the other hand, if a buyer declines to obtain an inspection, she likewise can't as easily come back later, because then you will say, "I told you to get it inspected. You chose not to; hence, you shouldn't complain."

Pitfalls in a Professional Home Inspection

Normally the inspection is requested in the purchase agreement. Indeed, most agreements today have language included in their boilerplate that calls for an inspection. You should watch out for at least three things to protect yourself:

 KEY CONCEPT *Normally the buyer pays for the home inspection.*

1. Time limit. Typically it's 14 days. You give the buyer two weeks to obtain and approve an inspection report. You probably shouldn't give longer unless there are unusual circumstances; otherwise, the buyer can simply delay the purchase.
2. Get a copy of the report with the right to show it to others. This is critical on two counts. The first is that you want to see what was found. Secondly, if this deal doesn't go through, you may be required to show subsequent buyers the report.
3. Refusal right on work required. You want to be able to choose whether and how to perform any repair work required. You don't want repairs to be automatic. For example, the report might conclude that your house needs a new roof at a cost of $15,000. You want to be able to decide whether to get a new roof, fix the existing roof, or simply not sell.

Who's the Inspector?

Since the buyer pays for the inspection and since it's the buyer who wants to discover problems, the buyer normally chooses the inspector. It's important to let the buyer do this. You don't want that buyer later on coming back and saying the inspector was biased because you chose him.

However, that doesn't mean that you should assume the inspector is all-knowing. She may range from expert to novice.

 KEY CONCEPT *While home inspectors are licensed in many states today, in others, almost anyone can hang out a shingle and call themselves a home inspector.*

You should ask if the inspector belongs to a trade organization. There are many major national organizations: National Association of Certified Home Inspectors (NACHI; *www.nachi.org*), American Society of Home Inspectors (ASHI; *www.ashi.com*), and National Association of Home Inspectors (NAHI; *www.nahi.org*) are three to consider.

There are also often trade organizations within your state. Ask the inspector if he belongs to one.

You should also ask if the inspector has any special training. Having previously been, for example, a county building inspector may especially qualify a person to be a professional home inspector. On the other hand, having previously simply been a carpenter may not. People with advanced credentials, such as structural or soils engineers, often make excellent home inspectors.

Should I Go Along on the Inspection?

Yes, certainly. You have every right to go. And there are at least two advantages to doing so.

First, if a problem is found, you can ask the inspector firsthand to describe it and to suggest various remedies. You may learn far more this way than later on getting a dry written report.

Secondly, the inspector may think there's a problem where one does not exist. For example, the inspector may see water on a wall and conclude that there's a leak somewhere. You might be able to inform the inspector that your child had a party yesterday and you just washed the wall to get some marks off. You could head off a big problem by being there and helping the inspector avoid drawing incorrect conclusions.

A side benefit is that you can learn a whole lot about not only your house but about the way homes are constructed and what to watch out for. This could aid you when you buy your next home.

Anticipate that the buyer will also come along, but don't be surprised if she doesn't. Most buyers simply don't make the time to go with the inspector and, thus, miss out on a lot of information that you'll get by being there.

What If the Inspector Finds Something Wrong?

Inspectors usually do. It's what they are paid to do. However, if the home is relatively new, the problems are usually minimal. Often they are nothing more than a broken light switch or a missing smoke detector.

If the report turns up items that total less than $100, don't even blink an eye. Either fix them or deduct the amount from the purchase price. It's when the report turns up something costing thousands of dollars that you need to pay special attention.

When serious money is involved, I follow this procedure:

1. Be sure you understand exactly what the inspector's report says. If it says the roof is leaking, that doesn't necessarily mean you need a new roof. It may mean you need to fix a leak. The difference is between $10,000 or more for a new roof and a couple of hundred dollars for a fix.
2. If the inspection says that something must be replaced (such as roof), demand a second opinion. Get a roofer out there, or two, or even three. Ask for alternatives to a whole-roof replacement. Will a patch do?
3. If it turns out that the expensive item must indeed be replaced, offer to share costs with the buyer. For example, a roof typically will last 25 years. If you've only lived in the house for the past 10, why should you pay for a whole new roof? Offer to pay a third of the cost. If the buyer balks, go for half.

4. Offer first to give a cash payment to the buyer (in the form of a price reduction) to cure a problem. That's the cleanest way. If the buyer refuses and insists that the work be done prior to closing escrow, insist that you select who does the work. Then get at least three estimates. You may find the prices differ enormously. If the buyer gets to select who does the work, you can be sure he will pick the highest bidder. If you get to select, you have the option of choosing the lowest.

5. If the issue is a health and safety concern, fix it. Don't refuse to fix a broken window or step. The buyer's falling or cutting herself in the first week could result in a lawsuit.

6. Do it yourself, if you want to, but only if it doesn't involved electrical, gas, or plumbing and if you're qualifed to do the work. The liability is too great. Also, consider how good a job you'll do. Remember, it has to look good for the buyer to finally approve it.

Some problems can't be avoided, particularly if your house is older. You may have simply not kept up with maintenance, and now it's come back to haunt you. It may simply be the case that to sell your house (to this buyer or to any buyer), you need to do some work. If that's the case, then you'll just have to bite the bullet and pay the costs.

What If the Buyer Wants to Renegotiate the Price?

Some buyers purposely hope that the professional home inspector will find something big wrong. They can then use this as a hammer to beat your price down. What should you do if you run up against this type of buyer?

Keep a cool head. Just remember that if you put the proper escape clause into your purchase agreement (you have the right to refuse to do any work), you're okay. You can always simply refuse to do the work.

Of course, this may mean that the buyers will walk. For example, if the heating system is shot, it costs upwards of $4,000 to fix, and you refuse to pay for it, the buyers could be well within their rights to dump the deal and move onto the next home.

KEY CONCEPT *Savvy buyers will always include a statement in the purchase agreement that says they have the right to approve or disapprove of the professional home inspection. And if they disapprove, they have the right to walk away from the deal with no strings attached and get their deposit back.*

Evaluate What the Buyers Are Demanding

Is the demand reasonable? To get back to our roof example, say your roof is, indeed, shot and must be replaced. Are they reasonably asking for a replacement roof just like the one you have? Or do they want an upgrade to tile or cement costing thousands more?

Do the buyers actually want the problem fixed, or are they looking for a price reduction instead? Maybe they are willing to live with the problem if you'll reduce the price.

Make a Counteroffer

Insist on an apple-for-apples repair and demand to only pay part of it, as noted above in the roof example.

Or offer a price reduction, but make it much less than the buyers want.

If the buyers are unwilling to compromise, then perhaps you'll want to walk. Sometimes the buyers are so set on "stealing" your property, they're unwilling to agree to a reasonable compromise. If that's the case, then simply bailing out of the deal may be your best strategy.

If you stick to your guns and refuse to budge, either the buyers will back down, in which case you'll get a good deal. Or they'll leave, in which case you'll avoid a bad deal.

Remember, a home inspection protects you as well as the buyer. There is really nothing to fear from it. The condition of your home is its condition. The inspection doesn't make it worse or better; it only helps reveal it. And if there are problems, you simply have to deal with them. Better to discover trouble early on and cure it when you have options than after the sale when the buyer's lawyer comes knocking.

Where Can I Get Disclosure Forms and a Home Inspection Report?

You can contact your state department of real estate via the Internet. (Just type your state and department of real estate, or whatever other name it may go by, into a search engine.) If your agency has its own disclosure form, it should send it to you. You can also ask a real estate agent if you can use the agency's form. The agent might balk at this, however, unless she hopes to get at least part of the action in the deal. Finally, some online sites provide disclosure forms. Check with Owners.com or FSBO.com.

Home inspectors are typically chosen by the buyers. However, you may want or need one on your own. They are listed in the yellow pages of the phone book, but your best source is online. (You can search on *home inspector* and your city.) However, a recommendation from a friend who has used one, or a friendly agent, can be helpful. Also, as with disclosure statements, some online sites that help owners sell homes have links to inspection organizations. And don't forget to check at the websites of the three big national trade organizations: *www. nachi.org, www.ashi.com, and www.nahi.org.*

13 Paperwork Solutions

IN MANY REAL estate transactions, the devil is in the paperwork. You may be excellent at finding a buyer, but then, suddenly, you can run into a brick wall. How do you handle the paperwork that solidifies the transaction?

 KEY CONCEPT *Contracts to purchase real estate must be in writing.— Statute of Frauds*

The big document in a transaction is the sales agreement. It's the backbone of the sale. (Sometimes it's called the "purchase agreement" or the "deposit receipt.") It needs to include all the terms and conditions of the sale.

In addition, the disclosure document, discussed in the last chapter; escrow papers; and myriad other documents are involved in the transaction. One way or another, when selling FSBO, you'll need to deal with all of these.

As I've suggested numerous times, you should get a professional to fill out the important documents for you. A fee-for-service agent or an attorney found on various by-owner websites can usually be counted on to provide the ultimate paperwork solution.

However, when it comes to that all-important sales agreement, you may find that to make a sale, you need to do the preliminary work yourself. That's what we'll discuss in this chapter.

What Goes into a Sales Agreement?

To understand how a sales agreement is put together today, a short jaunt into the past is helpful. When I started in real estate over 35 years ago in California, we didn't use a sales agreement. Instead, we used a deposit receipt. The deposit receipt, in fact, is still used in many areas.

A deposit receipt is just what it says it is: a receipt for a deposit on a piece of property, usually earnest money, that the buyer gives to the agent or the seller. Until the buyer puts up some earnest money or a deposit, you really don't have a solid deal. As part of the receipt, all the terms and conditions of the sale were specified. Hence, it became, in effect, a sales agreement.

Way back then, the deposit receipt was one legal page long. At the top, it contained space to fill in such obvious information as the correct address of the property, the name of the buyer, and the amount of the offer (purchase price).

Then a paragraph of legalese specified that the buyer was going to purchase the property according to the terms following, that "time was of the essence" (meaning the deal had to close by a certain date), and a few other conditions. About two-thirds of the remaining page consisted of blank lines. Someone—the seller, the buyer, or the agent—filled in all the terms.

Finally, there were places for all parties to sign and date the document at the bottom.

Keep in mind that the legal language on this simple document was only a few paragraphs. The agent, the seller, or the buyer filled in everything else by hand.

This old deposit receipt form served its function well. It was used to facilitate the sale of millions of pieces of property for decades. However, it had a serious flaw—in many cases, it wasn't legally binding.

A seller or a buyer who wanted to get out of the transaction for any reason without penalty frequently could go to court and demonstrate that the document wasn't really adequate. Either party could say that the agreement's language was vague or inaccurate or misrepresented their intentions.

Because the deposit receipt was mostly handwritten by agents, sellers, or buyers, and not by lawyers familiar with creating legally binding language, these contentions were often correct. In other words, the deposit receipt often was fatally flawed. It was rarely the legally binding document intended.

This placed a burden on agents. If either a buyer or a seller got out of a deal because of a flawed deposit receipt written by an agent, the party who felt injured often sued the agent. As a result, such lawsuits increased, and agents became gun-shy. When coupled with the skyrocketing price of real estate, the litigation began to involve serious money.

Band-Aid Fixes

To correct the situation, agents had their attorneys create sales agreements where more of the language was formally printed. Many of the paragraphs that the agents used to write in were now created by lawyers and included as part of the agreement. Instead of a single page of mostly blank lines, these new sales agreements were often two pages long with mostly printed text and only a few paragraphs where the agents would write in the terms of the sale.

The problem, of course, was that any time the agent, the seller, or buyer wrote in anything at all, there was a chance it wouldn't be legally binding because of incorrect language. By the 1970s, litigation had demonstrated that even these new contracts, with a minimum of inserted language, could prove to be a minefield. An innocuous-appearing sentence inserted at the time the sales agreement was signed could provide a way out for a buyer later on. The buyer might tie up the house for months only to walk away from the deal and be entitled to a full return of the deposit! Or, worse, even after the sale was consummated, the seller had moved out, and the buyer had moved in, inexact language in the contract and an angry buyer might result in litigation in which the seller was forced to pay damages to the buyer.

Today's Sales Agreement

This brings us to the present. Today the consensus seems to be that if it isn't written in by a lawyer, it isn't accurate or binding. Hence, we have the extraordinary situation in which agents are using sales agreements that are often

ten or more pages in length. The entire document is a preprinted form, and paragraphs for various contingencies are listed. All that the agent, buyer, or seller needs to do is write in the correct names of the parties involved and the property description, fill in the sales price and loan amount, and then check the appropriate paragraphs. No other writing on the document is recommended.

Furthermore, while state real estate groups usually prepare these forms for their agents/members to use, large real estate franchise companies, such as Coldwell-Banker or Century 21, have their attorneys prepare their own forms. Thus, there may be dozens of different formally prepared sales agreements used for real estate transactions, even within a given city.

The Plight of the FSBO

Needless to say, this puts a FSBO seller at a disadvantage. When you don't have your property listed, you don't get an agent's sales agreement. Yet to lock up a buyer, you do need a sales agreement that records a receipt for a deposit and spells out the terms of the sale. What do you do?

One answer used by some FSBO sellers, unwisely in my opinion, is to finesse the whole problem by simply going to their local stationery store and purchasing a form called something like "Sales Agreement for Real Property." A variety of these are put out by several publishing companies, and they contain all of the basics, although in truth, they tend to contain more blank space than legal language.

Other FSBO sellers may have a friend who is an agent from whom they ask to borrow a couple of sales agreement forms. Because most agents are eager to cooperate with FSBOs in any way, hoping that if the property doesn't sell, they will eventually get a listing, they cooperate and hand over some of the forms. Most agents, however, will first scrupulously cross the name of their company off the form, hoping to avoid any legal entanglements later on.

Now where does this leave the FSBO seller? In a sense, it leaves you not much better off than you were before. You have a form to use, but unless you're an attorney or very experienced in selling your own real estate (in which case you probably don't need this book), you still don't possess the knowledge to fill in the form correctly, even down to knowing which boxes to check and which to leave blank.

The fact remains that if you accept a buyer's deposit and write in the terms of the sale on a sales agreement (and do the job badly), you could be laying the groundwork for a lot of expensive litigation later on.

The Wrong Way, the Easy Way, the Right Way

This discussion is not intended to frighten you away from handling a FSBO sale because of the paperwork. It's intended only to present a background for some of the problems. There are, however, solutions—good ones.

The best solution, as suggested earlier, is not to attempt to handle the sales agreement at all (although you will want to write down the preliminary agreement with the buyer, as described shortly). Instead, have someone else who is a professional do it for you.

Using an agent comes to mind first. We've already covered the use of a fee-for-service agent and a discount broker for these purposes in an earlier chapter. So now let's move on to explain when and how to use an attorney for these services.

When to Use a Real Estate Attorney

In many states, attorneys who specialize in real estate abound. They make a living by handling the formalities of real estate transactions. Often they prepare the documents necessary to complete a deal.

Why not contact one of these attorneys *before* you find a buyer and work out an arrangement? The arrangement will go something like this: you will bring in a buyer who has agreed to purchase your home according to certain negotiated terms; the two of you will sit down, and the attorney will draw up the sales agreement; the buyer will then examine the document (and perhaps have her own attorney examine it); and then you will both sign it.

Simple? Easy? Quick? And it relieves you of the burden of having to worry about correctly filling out a sales agreement, something you probably can't do.

But what about the cost? Keep in mind that we're talking about an attorney who specializes in real estate transactions. Often these lawyers get as little as $500 to $1,500 for doing the documentary work related to a sale. Just be sure that you make an arrangement with the attorney before you need legal services.

Your lawyer may be able to give you clues about the information you will need to supply, so that when you come in, you will have all of it ready.

Dealing with a Nervous Buyer

Another advantage of using a fee-for-service agent, a discount broker, or an attorney is the help they can offer in dealing with a nervous buyer. One of the problems with selling FSBO is that buyers tend to be nervous. They tend to be wary of signing anything. Thus, even after you have a buyer who is ready, willing, and able to purchase your home, he may not want to commit directly to you. After all, the buyer may think, "How am I protected from an unscrupulous seller who wants to cheat me?"

Further, it is a rare buyer who is willing to give a deposit check directly to the seller. As buyers ought to know, once you receive that deposit check, it's your money. True, you might have to pay it back sometime in the future if the deal goes sour. However, until that time, you can stick the money in your account and spend it. If I were a buyer, the last thing in the world I would want to do would be to give my deposit directly to the seller.

Thus, the real estate agent or attorney provides a reasonable third party for the buyer. While buyers may question the validity of a document prepared by you, the seller, they are much more likely to have confidence in an agreement is drawn up by an agent or attorney. Furthermore, the buyer can question the agent or attorney and, presumably, get independent answers.

Finally, the buyer can turn the deposit over to the agent attorney, who may then turn it over to an escrow company after the purchase agreement is filled out and signed. In short, the attorney or agent becomes a great facilitator for you.

Don't Have an Escrow Officer Do the Work

We've already suggested one area that might be a minefield for you: filling out the sales agreement yourself without proper knowledge. Another is having someone who isn't really qualified do it, such as an escrow officer (or even an unqualified agent).

In the past, escrow officers were often obliging to sellers and buyers and would help them create a sales agreement. However, the purpose of escrow is to act as an independent third party in fulfilling the instructions of the sales agreement. While escrow officers are normally well versed in following instructions, they may be less than adequate in creating them.

As a result, some escrow officers have found themselves, painfully, at the center of disputes that came about from sales agreements they helped to create. Thus, to protect themselves, few escrow officers will help you with your sales agreement. Rather, after you have the agreement filled out and signed, they will simply aid you in seeing that its conditions are carried out.

Also, be careful of friends who are supposedly knowledgeable in real estate who offer to lend a helping hand. Your friend may, indeed, have successfully bought and sold a half dozen properties, but she may simply not have the very specific information needed for your particular transaction. That ignorance could get you in trouble.

What You Can Do Yourself

Okay, you've been warned about the problems. But you've found a buyer who's ready, willing, and able to purchase. It's time to sign a sales agreement with them. How, exactly, do you proceed?

Here's a method that any FSBO owner can follow that should end up with a solid sales agreement. Be sure to follow these five steps in order:

1. *Find a buyer.* You don't need to worry about signing an agreement until you have someone ready to sign. Get agreement on the terms. Having a buyer is one thing. Having a buyer who's ready, willing, and able to purchase at a price and terms for which you're willing to sell is something more. The next most important thing after finding a buyer is coming to an agreement with that buyer on price and terms.

2. *Write out a worksheet.* Many agents use a worksheet at this point, and you can too. It includes the areas that are negotiable. By going down the worksheet and filling in the blanks, you can quickly see if you and the buyer agree on the important points, as well as those you must negotiate. Seeing them on paper often clarifies issues that were foggy before. Don't sign the worksheet—it's not intended to be a legal document but rather just a guide.

3. *Take the worksheet to your agent or attorney.* From it, your attorney should be able to determine what the deal should look like and can then prepare a formal, written sales agreement.

4. *Sign the professional prepared agreement.* Have the buyer sign it and give you a check made payable to the attorney's escrow or a licensed escrow company.

5. *Take the check and the agreement to escrow.* Open an escrow account. You've just passed the biggest document hurdle!

Advantages of the Worksheet

The worksheet, as noted, helps to clarify the issues of the deal. It sets down in writing all of the things that you and the buyer agree upon.

Remember: Nobody signs it. But just getting things down in writing is important. Often when two people speak, particularly two who may be in an adversarial relationship such as buyer and seller, they misunderstand each other. You may say something that the buyer misinterprets as a concession and vice versa. The whole point of doing the worksheet is that you and the buyer can sit down together and put in writing exactly what the terms of the sale are.

Furthermore, because neither you nor the buyer is actually going to sign this worksheet and because by itself it's not any sort of a binding agreement, it is extremely useful as a negotiating tool. There may be some point of disagreement between you and the buyer—perhaps the matter of the down payment or the interest rate on a loan you are carrying back. You can reasonably say to the buyer, "Let's sit down and see if we can work it out on paper. This is just a worksheet. I'm not going to sign it and neither are you. We'll just put the numbers down and see if we can work it out."

Once you've set the price and terms down, you and the buyer together can take the worksheet to an attorney or agent who can correctly fill out a sales agreement based on what you've agreed upon.

Creating a Worksheet

On the following page is a worksheet that I have found to be helpful. Keep in mind that we're only talking about a worksheet here, not a sales agreement. It's usually best to do it in pencil so you can erase and change things as you go along.

If you and the buyer are in disagreement on several points, sometimes it's helpful to do two worksheets—one for you and one for the buyer. Then you can attempt to reconcile them. Or if you can't accomplish a reconciliation yourselves, perhaps the agent or attorney to whom you take the worksheets to can help you come to terms.

 K E Y   C O N C E P T *Do* not *have anyone sign the worksheet. It's not intended to be a binding agreement.*

And that's all there is to it. The worksheet becomes a tool for trying out different ideas and numbers. Using the worksheet, you may be able to construct a deal with a buyer that you might otherwise lose.

Be Sure You Understand the Worksheet

Because the worksheet is the most important tool you may have when it comes time to hammer out the price and terms, you should be clear on what areas you should get preliminary agreement. Let's take it one step at a time.

Sales Price. Most people start here, and it is a good idea to get at least an offering price down. However, often the sales price comes about as the result of a combination of how much money the buyer can put down and how big a mortgage she can negotiate. Put down an offering price, but be sure it's in pencil so that you can scratch it out as negotiations continue.

Deposit. Sellers usually want a big deposit because they know that the bigger the deposit, the bigger the buyer's commitment to the deal. Buyers, on the other hand, often want a lower deposit, because it means they are tying up less money.

FSBO Purchase Worksheet

*(**NOT** INTENDED TO BE A LEGALLY BINDING DOCUMENT!)*

Address of property

Buyer's name

Seller's name

Price $_____

Deposit $_____

Cash down $_____ (in addition to deposit)

First mortgage $_____

    Assume _____?   New _____?

    Interest rate _____%

    Fixed _____?   Adj. _____?

    Term _____?   Pts. _____?

Second mortgage $_____

    Assume _____?   New _____?

    Interest rate _____%

    Fixed _____?   Adj. _____?

    Term _____?   Pts. _____?

Third mortgage $_____

    Assume _____?   New _____?

    Interest rate _____%

    Fixed _____?   Adj. _____?

    Term _____?   Pts. _____?

Total $_____ (must equal price)

Other conditions of sale that are desired:_____

_____

_____

The desired date the escrow will close _____

The desired date the buyer gets occupancy_____

The real estate attorney to be used_____

The escrow company to be used_____

There is no rule on how big the deposit should be. It should be large enough, however, to convince you that the buyer is serious. Many agents have a hard-and-fast rule that the deposit should be $5,000, regardless of the purchase price. However, that hardly makes sense on lower-priced properties and may be insufficient on higher-priced ones. Here's a schedule of how big a deposit I usually want from a buyer when I am selling a house.

Deposit Schedule

To $50,000	$1,000 minimum up to 5%
$50,000 to $100,00	$2,000 minimum up to 3%
$100,000 to $300,000	$3,000 minimum up to 3%
More than $300,000	$5,000 minimum up to 3%

Keep in mind that the deposit is the money you may be entitled to receive if the buyer can't complete the transaction. If the sales agreement is properly drawn and the buyer doesn't perform as promised through no fault of your own, you may get the money. In the real world, however, extenuating circumstances often allow the buyer to back out of the deal and get his money back. Don't make the mistake of aiming for the deposit.

 KEY CONCEPT *Your goal is not to get the deposit; it is to sell your house.*

Mortgages. This is the trickiest area for most people. If you're like most FSBO sellers, you know something, but not a great deal, about financing a real estate purchase. Thus, you may feel inadequate dealing with the issue of mortgages.

However, because virtually all real estate transactions are financed (few people pay cash these days), you'll have to know at least enough to get by.

We'll cover much of what you need to know in the next chapter. For now, let's say that you can help the buyer by at least jotting down the amount of the mortgage(s), the estimated interest rate, points, term, and type (fixed or adjustable rate).

Note: It is important that when you jot down items such as interest rate and points (points, by the way, represent percentage points of the mortgage amount; in other words, three points on a $100,000 mortgage is equal to $3,000), you list them at a higher level than you can reasonably expect to get at the current time. The reason is that these rates fluctuate. You don't want to lose a buyer because interest rates jumped up half a percent or points jumped between the time you hammered out the agreement and the sale was ready to close.

Terms. This, of course, is the trickiest area of all. As noted earlier, this is the area where agents got into trouble in the past. If you don't try to add a bunch of legalese, however, and leave the actual writing of the terms to your attorney, you shouldn't have much of a hassle in this area.

Terms may include such items as the following:

- *How long does the buyer have to qualify for the mortgage?* You don't want to take your property off the market unless you're sure the buyer will qualify. Typically, the buyer is entitled to a full refund of the deposit if she can't get the mortgage. You may want to have your attorney specify that the buyer has a week to get preliminary loan approval or four weeks for final loan approval.
- *What personal property will be included in the sale?* Typically, buyers want the attorney to specify that all flooring, window covering, and fixtures are included. However, you may want it specified that a favorite ceiling lamp in the dining room, for example, is not included in the sale.
- *Must any conditions be met before the sale can be completed?* Buyers may want "subject to" or contingency clauses included by the attorney. They may, for example, insist that the sale be subject to their recreational vehicle's fitting along the side of the house. You may allow them a day or two to take measurements to be sure.

  On the other hand, they may insist the attorney specify that the sale is contingent upon the sale of their current home. You may not want to tie up your property waiting for them to sell theirs, or you may insist that, yes, you'll give them right of first refusal on a sale provided that you can keep your house on the market. The term "right of first refusal" usually means that in the event you find a cash buyer before the buyers who made the first offer sell their current home, they have a set time, typically 72 hours, to remove the contingency or lose the deal.

- *What inspections, if any, are you going to have?* In the past, there used to be one basic inspection—for termites and fungus infestations. The reason for this inspection was that most lenders required a clearance before they would fund a mortgage. In recent years, however, many things have changed, not the least of which are inspections. Today, a wise seller insists that the buyer has the home inspected by a competent building inspector. Re-read the previous chapter if you're not sure about this.
- Note: Insisting that buyers have inspections is also a selling feature. If you, the FSBO seller, agree to an inspection, most buyers will feel that you're not trying to hide anything.
- *Are there any other terms?* Everything in real estate is negotiable. Your buyer may wish to have the attorney insert some strange condition that you've never heard of. If you agree, jot it down. Remember, anything can be included in this worksheet. However, your real estate attorney should advise you about the wisdom of the particular terms you and the buyer want inserted.

And so forth. The terms can consist of almost anything. Your goal here is not to write them in legalese but to get them down as clearly and succinctly as possible so that both you and the buyer know what the terms are. Let the agent or attorney handle the written details.

 KEY CONCEPT *Try to have as few terms as possible and make those few as short as possible. The more terms you have, the greater your chance of losing the deal through a misunderstanding or disagreement.*

Include Dates. All real estate transactions are based on performance over time. You should be willing to give the buyer a reasonable amount of time to arrange a loan. However, you don't want the transaction to drag on interminably. Typically, financing can be arranged in 45 days. Therefore, you will want to agree with the buyer on a date for the close of escrow and the time when the title will transfer and you'll get your sale and money.

Keep in mind that while you will agree to this date, it can be flexible. Things can happen that can cause delays, including financing problems on the buyer's part or, perhaps, difficulties in clearing title on your part. However, the date is what you will be aiming at. Your attorney will want to add language explaining what will happen to the deposit in the event the sale doesn't close by the appointed date or if it doesn't close at all. (See the previous section on deposits.)

The date of occupancy or when the buyer takes possession of the property is often the same date as the close of escrow, but it doesn't have to be. It can be any date you and the buyer agree upon. For example, the buyer may want to get into the house earlier or later.

However, in most cases you would be wise not to let the buyer occupy the property until the deal has closed and title has transferred. The reason, simply, is that if the buyer takes possession of the property and then, for any reason, can't close the deal, you not only haven't sold your house, but you've got someone in it whom you now may have to go to court to evict!

Include Names. It's a good idea to name the real estate agent or attorney you're planning to use as well as the title insurance company and the escrow company that you will use in the transaction. Because the buyer will be filling out this worksheet with you, you will quickly discover if he has any preferences. If so, you may wish to accede to them, particularly in the case of escrow and title companies.

Note: The Real Estate Settlement Procedures Act (RESPA) may prohibit you as a seller from insisting on a particular title insurance or escrow company.

You will, however, probably want to insist on the real estate attorney or agent who has already agreed to write up the deal. If the buyer insists on using her own attorney or agent, then you may want to arrange a meeting at which both will be present, your attorney/agent and the buyer's.

The Bottom Line

In this chapter, we've looked at how to get the documentation for a real estate transaction handled when you're selling by owner. Remember, don't try to take the "easy route" of filling out a document you purchase at a stationery store or even online on your own. The written documents are the backbone of every real estate deal. Get them drawn up properly by a professional.

14 | Seller Financing to Help Make the Sale

SURE, IT WOULD really be nice if a buyer came in and offered to pay for your home in cash. But don't expect that to happen any time soon.

Almost all residential real estate is financed, which means your buyer likely will need a mortgage. The trouble is that many buyers are illiterate about financing. They don't know a thing about getting a loan. So if you want a sale, it's up to you to help them.

The big thing with financing is to determine as quickly as possible whether or not this buyer can actually afford to purchase your home. That's what agents do when they qualify buyers. As a by-owner seller, it's up to you to do this important task.

Find Out If the Buyer Is Qualified to Purchase Your Home

A good rule of thumb is that many people who look at your house can't really afford to buy it. Of course, the lower your home is priced and the higher the typical income in your area, the more people will be able to afford it. The higher your price and the lower the typical income, the fewer can afford it.

What this means is that when you eventually get someone who says he is ready and willing to purchase, your first move must be to determine if he or she really can do so. It may turn out that the thrill of getting a buyer will fade rapidly when you discover that the buyer has bad credit, doesn't have enough income, or hasn't got a big enough bank account to make the purchase.

Of course, it's up to a lender (assuming you're not doing seller financing, discussed shortly) to make the determination. Today, that's relatively easy.

How Do I Broach Credit-Worthiness and Income with a Buyer?

Because you are the seller, many buyers will hesitate to reveal necessary financial information directly to you. They probably feel their personal finances are none of your business. And to some extent, they are right.

However, you do have a right to learn if they can finance your purchase. The real trick is to get the information without scaring the buyers away. Therefore, you should not come out and ask direct questions, such as "How much money do you have in the bank?" or "Do you have any bad credit?" The buyers may decide that you're too nosy and may take their business elsewhere.

On the other hand, I suggest that you do drop hints early on about what it takes to buy your home. For example, as the buyers begin to show significant interest, you can explain that if they plan to put 20 percent down, their payments at then-current interest rates will likely be around $X per month. If they put 10 percent down, the monthly moves up to $X a month. At 5 percent down it's even more. All *plus* taxes and insurance.

You can watch their reactions. Do they seem to feel that's acceptable? Or do they blink, look astonished, and give the impression that it's an impossibly high figure? If the latter, I wouldn't start sending out change-of-address notices quite yet.

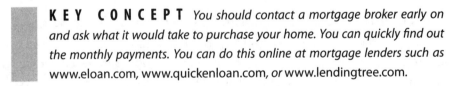

KEY CONCEPT *You should contact a mortgage broker early on and ask what it would take to purchase your home. You can quickly find out the monthly payments. You can do this online at mortgage lenders such as www.eloan.com, www.quickenloan.com, or www.lendingtree.com.*

Once the buyers appear interested and seem ready to make an offer, I suggest you then ask, "Are you pre-approved?"

Has the Buyer Been Pre-Approved?

Pre-approval is exceedingly common in today's market place. The buyer goes to a lender, usually a physical or an online mortgage broker, and fills out a standard mortgage application.

Then the broker submits the form to a lender who runs a credit check, and finally, if done correctly, runs the whole thing by underwriters. With today's computers and electronic hookups, the answer quickly comes back saying how big a monthly payment the buyer can afford and how big a mortgage that translates into. This is put into a letter that the buyer can hand to you.

If your buyer has been pre-approved, ask to see the pre-approval letter. This should not be painful for the buyer in the least since it doesn't contain any information about the buyer's financial situation. Rather it should contain, if not the maximum mortgage the buyer can get, then at the least the maximum monthly payment he can afford. And from that, any amortization table can quickly get you to the maximum price, given the current interest rates. (Amortization tables are widely available online at most mortgage lending websites, such as those noted above.)

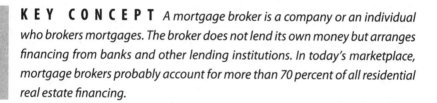

KEY CONCEPT *A mortgage broker is a company or an individual who brokers mortgages. The broker does not lend its own money but arranges financing from banks and other lending institutions. In today's marketplace, mortgage brokers probably account for more than 70 percent of all residential real estate financing.*

What If the Buyers Aren't Pre-Approved?

If the buyers say they don't have pre-approval, then you can suggest they get it. You can point out that they'll need it no matter what home they try to buy, yours or someone else's. And, hopefully, you've done your homework so you can recommend a mortgage broker who can quickly check their income and credit and get pre-approval.

If the buyers aren't pre-approved, then it's not unreasonable, as noted, to ask them to go through the process. But perhaps you want to tie them into the purchase before then by signing a sales agreement (see the last chapter for suggestions on how to accomplish this). If they say they're sure they can get a mortgage, it's not unreasonable to demand a clause in the agreement that asks them to prove it. This clause says the buyers will be pre-approved by a lender within a reasonably short amount of time, say a few days. If they don't get such firm pre-approval (defined shortly), then the deal is null and void.

Remember, if they can't get financing and you go forward with the sale, you could be taking your house off the market and tying it up, perhaps for months, before finding out they really can't buy.

If the buyers protest the clause, I suggest that you explain the problem to them in exactly those terms. They now want to buy and are probably eager to do so. You've agreed on a price. However, before you agree to take your house off the market for an extended period of time, you need to know that they can get necessary financing. It's not a bit unreasonable.

Don't Get Pushy

Beyond following the suggestions provided above, I caution that you not go any further in financially qualifying your buyers. If they have a legitimate pre-approval letter for enough to buy your home, it's not quite like money in the bank, but it's darn close. If they have a firm commitment pre-approval letter (explained below), get started on the worksheet outlined in the last chapter and reach agreement on terms and price. Take it to your agent or attorney to have a formal sales agreement drafted and signed…and you're on your way to a sale. (Be sure the agreement specifies a time limit for the buyers to get approval for *funding* of their mortgage.)

A Lender's Firm Pre-Approval Commitment Is Better

While most general pre-approval letters are indeed nice, they are not a guarantee. Most of them say the same thing, namely that *if* the buyer's credit and employment don't change, and *if* they have the money in the bank that they claim, then they probably can get a loan.

What you would ideally like is a firmer commitment by a lender. This is a bit different. It says that the lender (not the mortgage broker but the company actually lending the mortgage money) has checked out not only the buyer's credit but verified their income/employment and their money on deposit. It says that it will commit to giving them a mortgage. (Of course, extenuating circumstances, such as a job loss or illness, can quash even a firm commitment pre-approval.)

A general pre-approval letter is a good start. But you can just about take a firm commitment pre-approval to the bank. To learn the difference, read the pre-approval letter carefully. Does it simply say that the buyers are pre-approved? Or does it commit the lender to actually making a loan?

Can't I Just Approve the Buyers Myself?

Not if they're getting an institutional loan (in other words, a loan not from you). Today, getting "approved" means the buyers pass strict underwriting requirements from either a direct lender, such as a bank, or a secondary lender, such as Fannie Mae or Freddie Mac. Whether or not you yourself approve of the buyers is irrelevant when getting an institutional loan. It's whether the institutions agree to lend money to the buyers that counts.

What If I'm Doing My Own Financing?

KEY CONCEPT *When offering or denying credit, you may find you're required by federal or state law to make certain declarations to the would-be borrower. All of which is a good reason to check with an attorney in your state who is knowledgeable on seller financing before moving forward with it.*

This a different story. If you're offering seller financing—a second mortgage—as part of the purchase price, then you have every right to approve the buyer's credit personally. After all, now you're the lender.

Getting a pre-approval letter is nice. But if you're doing the financing, chances are the buyers don't have it. (If they did, they probably wouldn't need your financing.)

Have the buyer fill out a qualification sheet, such as the one on the following pages , and get a credit report. You can use these to qualify buyers who are asking you for seller financing. The qualification sheet should ask a minimum of information yet give you a good idea of whether your buyer is likely to be able to pay back your loan.

 KEY CONCEPT *Seller financing means that you "lend" the buyer a portion of your equity in the property, typically in the form of a second mortgage. (The first mortgage usually comes from an institutional lender.)*

How to Use a "Buyer Qualification Chart"

If the buyers fill out the buyer qualification chart even partially, you may get enough information to determine quickly if they qualify for the loan they are requesting from you. Keep in mind, however, that you can only request this information—you can't demand it. If the buyers refuse, then you may simply not want to give them seller financing.

Chart Explanation

Monthly Gross Income. Most buyers won't hesitate to tell you their monthly gross income. They usually understand that income is critical to buying a property, and they will want to let you know that they make enough to qualify.

What you need to know is that all of their mortgage payments, including any "first" they'll get from the lender as well as a "second" from you plus taxes and insurance, should not equal more than about a third of their total gross income. Lenders' studies indicate that often if the total house payments are higher than this ratio, there's a better chance the borrower won't be able to make the payments. If that happens, you might have to foreclose and take the property back.

If your buyers indicate sufficient income, don't rejoice quite yet. Keep in mind that from total income, lenders subtract any long-term payments (typically those lasting four months or longer) that the borrowers may have. These include payments for cars, credit cards, alimony, and loans. If they're in debt up

FIGURE 14.1 Buyer Qualification Chart

Name _____

Address _____

Phone number _____

Income _____

What is your monthly gross income?

    Husband $ _____

    Wife $ _____

    Other source $ _____

    Total $ _____

What are the monthly payments on your long-term debt, including:

    Car payments $ _____

    Credit cards $ _____

    Alimony $ _____

    Loans $ _____

    Other $ _____

    Less total $ _____

    Total income available $ _____

Credit History

YES NO

☐   ☐   Do you have any foreclosures?

☐   ☐   Did you file for bankruptcy in the past 10 years?

☐   ☐   Did you have any delinquent loans in the past 7 years?

☐   ☐   Do you know of any credit problems you may have?

continued on next page

FIGURE 14.1 Buyer Qualification Chart (Continued)

Cash to Make Down Payment

The cash required to purchase this home, including closing costs, is $_____

YES NO

☐ ☐ Do you have this money in checking/savings?

☐ ☐ Do you have it another source such as a CD?

☐ ☐ Are you borrowing it from relatives? Will they cosign the loan?

☐ ☐ Are you borrowing it from a bank or other lender?

☐ ☐ May I call your employer to verify your income?

☐ ☐ May I contact your bank to verify your benefit(s)?

Buyer's signature_____

---

to their ears elsewhere, even with a high income, they may not be able to make your payments.

Ask If You Can Get a Credit Report. After all, it's the minimum that any institutional lender would demand. Be sure you get written permission from the buyers; else it may not be legitimate for you to seek such information. You can ask the buyers to get one for you – they can easily do this through any of the major credit reporting bureaus. You can also usually get one through a real estate agent or directly through a variety of credit reporting services on the Internet (for a fee), such as *www.tenantverification.com* and *www.e-renter.com*.

If the buyers are reluctant to allow you to obtain a credit report, they may have credit problems. If so, you want to get that out into the open. If you're concerned that your buyers may be hiding some information, you can point out that every institutional lender will run a complete three-bureau credit check, which will reveal all of this information anyway.

When you obtain a credit report, look to see how frequently the prospective buyer has missed payments or made late payments and for any bankruptcies and foreclosures. All of these (especially the last two) suggest this person isn't likely to go the extra mile to make new payments.

What If My Buyers Answer Yes to Foreclosures and Bankruptcies?
Answering yes to any or all of the questions shouldn't automatically disqualify a buyer from getting a loan. Most institutional lenders accept reasonable explanations, so you may want to too. For example, a foreclosure may show up that was really for someone else with a similar name. In my own case, a foreclosed mortgage showed up for a property I had sold five years earlier. I simply presented my settlement papers for the deal, which showed that the buyer had assumed the mortgage when I sold the property and the foreclosure wasn't in my name, and the troubles went away.

However, if your buyers answer yes to the first two questions (foreclosure and bankruptcy) without having a good explanation, you could be in trouble. Most lenders simply won't consider them, so why should you?

What About Delinquencies and Slow or Missed Payments?
Delinquent loans and late payments are less condemning but nonetheless troublesome. If a good explanation is provided, again, you may want to overlook them. For example, a bout of illness could account for late payments or delinquencies on a number of loans five years ago. However, if the borrower got well, made them all good, and has been current ever since, it's unlikely a lender would deny a mortgage because of the problem. Again, why should you?

However, what should you do if your buyers reveal a serious credit problem? My suggestion is that you state your doubts about their ability to make payments and, unless they can satisfy you with a reasonable explanation, forgo lending them money. Selling your house to a borrower who is a bad financial risk may mean you'll face lots of trouble down the road.

What About the Buyers' Down Payment?
The final qualifying questions are designed to reveal the source of the buyers' down payment. You don't really care where they're getting it, as long as it isn't borrowed. The rule is that borrowed money should not be used as a down payment for the purchase of a home, as it increases the total payments and decreases the buyer's commitment to the property.

Consider, if the buyer puts 20 or even 10 percent down, she will surely want to keep that property, if at all possible, out of foreclosure. But how serious will that commitment be if the buyer's putting in none if her money?

What Kind of Financing Should You Look for from a Buyer?

Thus far, we've been looking at finding a buyer who can afford to purchase your home. Now let's consider the types of financing that this buyer might obtain. You need to know a little about financing to talk intelligently to your buyer and steer him in the right direction.

All Cash to You

Essentially, this means that the buyer gets a new first mortgage from an institution, such as a savings and loan association or a bank, for a portion of the purchase price, typically 80–95 percent, and then pays cash for the balance of 5–20 percent. This is the ideal way to sell your home because you get all cash. (That's assuming, of course, that you want all cash. Some sellers prefer to get a portion of the sales price in the form of a mortgage. We'll cover that in the next section.)

You should be aware that for all conventional loans above 80 percent loan-to-value (LTV), the borrower must pay an additional premium for private mortgage insurance (PMI), which protects the lender against default. This adds to the borrower's payments. (For FHA loans, that premium is usually built into the loan itself.)

Seller-Assisted Financing

We've already touched on how to qualify a buyer for seller financing. Now let's cover some of the advantages and pitfalls in offering such financing to your buyer.

For most sellers, a perfect world would see all buyers put down cash on a new loan. In the real world, many buyers simply don't have enough cash for the down payment. Thus, buyers may ask you to assist them in making the purchase. In a down market, doing so can be very important to helping make a sale.

Should you assist with seller financing? It can be risky. But often the answer comes down to something as simple as this: to make the sale, you may have to help with the financing.

You may find that you get lots of lookers coming through your property. Some are real buyers who would like to purchase, but no one seems to have the requisite cash and credit to make the purchase.

After a period of having your house on the market, you may decide that you have to do something to try to convert those would-be buyers to real buyers. That something may be helping them with the financing. If they don't qualify for a full new mortgage, perhaps they'll qualify for part, and you can lend them the other part. If they have enough for a down payment, you can finance part of the down.

Should You Offer a Second Mortgage? The most common form of seller-assisted financing is the second mortgage. Here, instead of getting all cash, you take back a mortgage for a portion of the sales price. For example, the buyers may have 10 percent cash to put down but can qualify only for an 80 percent mortgage, so you carry the remaining balance of 10 percent of the purchase price:

> 80 percent institutional mortgage
> 10 percent second mortgage
> 10 percent cash
> _____
> 100 percent total purchase price

There may be some advantages for you here. For example, you may get a relatively high interest rate, compared with sticking the same money in the bank. The bank may pay only 4 or 5 percent, but the second mortgage might be for 9 or 10 percent. That could mean a big return.

On the other hand, there are disadvantages. If the buyer defaults for any reason and doesn't make the payments, your only recourse might be to foreclose on your second mortgage and take the property back.

This can be an expensive proposition. The foreclosure process, depending on your state, can take months—even up to almost a year. There probably will be back payments on both your second and on the first mortgage to make up during that time (you'll want to keep up the payments on the first to be sure it doesn't foreclose first and eliminate your interest in the property), plus taxes, insurance, and the costs of foreclosure.

In addition, once you get the property back, it may be in terrible shape and require major fixing up.

My own feeling with regard to second mortgages is that if I help the buyer by providing one, I don't count it as money gained. Rather, I just forget about it. If the buyer pays regularly and eventually pays it off, I regard it as a boon. If the buyer doesn't make payments, I then have to decide whether or not it's worthwhile to foreclose. In some cases, it may simply be better to forget the debt because the costs of foreclosure are too great. (Hopefully you're able to sell for a high enough price that the second mortgage was gravy.)

In other cases, foreclosure makes sense, particularly when there's lots of equity in the property, prices have appreciated, and there's a profit to be made.

If you're being asked to offer seller-assisted financing in the form of a second mortgage, you must decide whether the risk is worthwhile to you. If you are getting a high enough price or if you're desperate to sell, you may go along with seller financing.

My suggestion remains, however: don't think of it as money in the bank. The world of second mortgages is fraught with problems and pitfalls.

To help you estimate the actual risk involved, consider the information in figure 14.2.

 K E Y   C O N C E P T *The more the buyer puts down in cash, the safer your second mortgage.*

What About Nothing-Down Offers?

When you sell FSBO (and even when you have an agent!), you can expect to get all kinds of offers, many of which may be totally wacky. But unless you are careful, you may not distinguish the bad offers from the good. One of the most common offers you are likely to receive is the offer of no down payment at all.

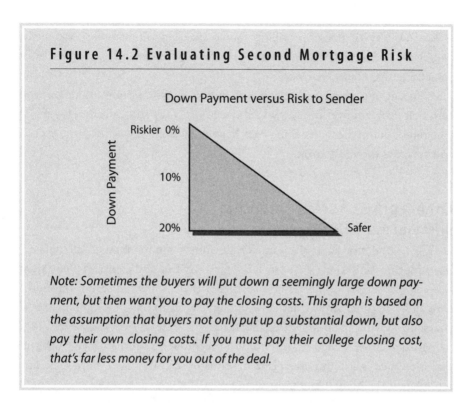

Figure 14.2 Evaluating Second Mortgage Risk

Down Payment versus Risk to Sender

Riskier 0%

10%

20%

Safer

Down Payment

Note: Sometimes the buyers will put down a seemingly large down payment, but then want you to pay the closing costs. This graph is based on the assumption that buyers not only put up a substantial down, but also pay their own closing costs. If you must pay their college closing cost, that's far less money for you out of the deal.

Here, the buyers not only offer you nothing down but may also want you to pay all of the closing costs. As an enticement, these buyers may offer you full price or even higher.

The seller who accepts such a nothing-down offer is usually one who is blinded by price and overlooks the reality of the deal. Remember, buyers who put no cash into a deal have no strong commitment to make monthly payments or to keep up the property. Such buyers may simply be out to resell for a profit as soon as possible. What's worse, they may attempt to "rape the property." That means they rent it out for as long as they can get away with it, collecting the rents and not making any payments to you. If and when you foreclose, you may find a tenant in the property who refuses to move—or a home that has been wrecked.

If you sell nothing down and the market is going up, you might still come out okay. But if the market's down, you may find it costs more to foreclose than the home is worth. In which case, you'll probably just walk and take a loss.

To my way of thinking, selling for no down payment is just asking for trouble. You are, in effect, delaying your current problem and exchanging it for something that could be worse.

Your current problem is selling your home. By selling nothing down, you turn that problem over to someone else who really doesn't care about you and who might dump the whole thing back in your lap later, only with far more costs and expenses for you to bear.

Other Forms of Seller Financing
Offer the Buyer a First Mortgage

The second mortgage, although it is the most common form of seller financing, is not the only kind. If you own the property free and clear and if you want a steady income at an interest rate far higher than you could secure through a bank, CD, or other similar device, you might want to handle *all* the financing yourself by giving the buyer a first mortgage.

Mortgages are valued in order of their recordation on the property. A second mortgage is a higher mortgage in terms of security than a third. The first mortgage is the highest and most secure of all. Of course, to offer a first, you'd either have to own the property free and clear, as noted above, or pay off any existing mortgages yourself.

If you decide to offer a first, be sure that you go through the same procedures as for a second, although you might want to insist on a buyer with better credit. I suggest you always get a credit report, verify income, and be sure buyers put down at least 10 percent plus closing costs in cash.

Lease Option

Here, instead of selling, you rent out your home to a potential buyer on a long-term lease, usually for a couple of years. The buyer often pays a higher rent with a portion of it to be applied in the future to a down payment. The buyer has the option of eventually purchasing the property. You can often get the majority of your money out by refinancing on your own before lease optioning.

If you get a lot of option money up front, say 5 percent of the ultimate pur-chase price, and if the buyer continues to make payments on time and eventually purchases, the lease option can be an excellent method of selling a property.

However, too often the tenant/buyer doesn't want to put up much option money, perhaps none. Too often the tenant/buyer, after paying on half the term of the lease, discovers he won't really be able to buy and begins paying late, lets the property go, and eventually abandons it.

In the worst case, the lessee/buyer won't pay and won't leave, and you have to initiate eviction proceedings. Eviction, however, is made more difficult because the option, at least in theory, gives the tenant/buyer some slight own-ership interest in the property. Eviction could take you longer and could be more expensive under a lease option than under a standard lease.

My suggestion is to be very careful with the lease option and remember that it's not a sale. It's converting your home-for-sale into a rental with a hoped-for sale sometime in the future. For more information on the lease option, check out my book *Rent to Own*.

 KEY CONCEPT *In some states, lease options are strictly regu-lated. Be sure to check with a local attorney before attempting to offer one on your property.*

The Best Rule I Have Found

Never assist with financing unless the buyer agrees to an arm's-length pur-chase, puts at least 10 percent down, and pays in cash for the majority of the closing costs. You might lose some sales by insisting on these conditions. But the one you make is more likely to stick.

15 Taxes You May Owe on the Sale

WILL YOU NEED to pay taxes on the sale of your home?

Maybe. A lot depends on how long you lived there and how big your profit was.

If your net selling price is more than your tax basis (usually what you paid for the property), the difference is called a capital gain, and tax may be owed on it.

That would certainly be the case if the property were a rental or investment property. But if it was your home, is there still a capital gains tax?

There may be, but you may not have to pay it. A different set of rules apply to principal residences. Provided you meet the criteria, you can exclude a very large portion of your gain from taxes, up to $250,000 a person ($500,000 for a married couple filing jointly).

That means you can, if you qualify and depending on your home's price, take the money and run—sell your home and pocket the profit without paying taxes on it.

Sound too good to be true? This is one case where it really is true. Of course, the catch is qualifying, and that's what we'll consider in this chapter.

KEY CONCEPT **Caution:** *The following tax discussion should be considered an overview of an extremely complex subject. Be aware that the tax laws are in a constant state of flux, being changed by Congress, the courts, and IRS interpretations. What you read here today may be untrue tomorrow. Therefore, do not rely on this material. Before taking any action with tax consequences, consult with a competent tax professional.*

What Is the Exclusion?

The Taxpayers Relief Act of 1997 provided a new exclusion of up to $250,000 per person on the sale of a main home, or up to $500,000 when a married couple filing jointly sells their home.

For example, let's say that your capital gain is $400,000. As a married couple filing jointly and otherwise qualifying, you pay no tax. On the other hand, if you're a qualifying single person with a $400,000 gain, the first $250,000 is excluded, and you pay taxes on the remaining balance of $150,000.

There Are Many Benefits—and Requirements
You Can Take the Exclusion Up to Once Every Two Years

If you sell and buy a main home today, then two years from today, you can sell that new home and claim the exclusion all over again. You can claim the full exclusion as many times as you want, as long as you own and reside in each main home for a minimum of two years.

Further, you don't need to invest that money in another house (as was the case before). You can use it any way you want: to buy a boat or a car, take a vacation, or blow it in Vegas. It's your money to do with as you wish.

There Is a Two-Year Qualifying Period

The rule is that the home must be your personal residence for the previous two out of five years. Thus, as along as you can come up with 24 months out of the previous 60 during which you actually lived in the property and otherwise qualify, you can take the exclusion.

In Some Cases, the Qualifying Two-Year Period Doesn't Apply

A seldom talked about part of the tax law exclusion provides that if you change the location of your employment, a health condition requires you to sell, or an unforeseen circumstance occurs that mandates the sale, you may not be required to have kept the home for the full two-year period to get at least a part of the exclusion.

While the interpretation of this part of the law is in a gray area, it appears to be quite liberal. A wide variety of reasons may be acceptable for an early sale.

Further, the amount of the exclusion you can claim under this provision, as of this writing, appears to be 1/24th for each month you actually lived in the property. In other words, if you lived in the property for only 12 months, you'd get half, or up to $125,000. Check with your tax professional for more details.

The Home Must Be Your Principal Residence

What is a principal residence? To qualify for the exclusion, the property must be your main home; that is, where you live most of the time. The government gives a lot of leeway as to what that means. Your principal residence can be your house, condo, or other type of home. A trailer home has been considered a personal residence, as has a house boat!

It's important to understand, however, what *principal residence* really means. It has to be where you reside most of the time. It has to be truly your home.

A lot of confusion occurs with regard to rentals. Can a rental be a personal residence? Obviously, for purposes of the exclusion, if you're the tenant, the answer is no.

But what if you're the landlord? Let's say that you own a duplex (or "duet," as it's called in some parts of the country) and live in one side while you rent out the other. Is the duplex your principal residence?

Yes and no. Strictly speaking, only half of it is. The part in which you reside is your principal residence. The part that you rent out is investment property. For purposes of the exclusion, half of any gain should be subject to the rule, while the part of the gain coming from the rental side should be subject to capital gains taxes in the year the property is sold.

What happens if, after living in your home for many years, you move and rent it out, then later you decide to sell. Is it still your principal residence? This was a gray area in the past, but the new rule has helped to clear this up. Remember, you only have to have been living in the property for two out of the previous five years. That means you could have rented the property out for three of those years. On the other hand, if you rented it out for four years of the previous five, you're probably out of luck.

Should you move back in before selling? It's something you may want to consider, depending on your situation. If you've rented it out for too long to qualify for the two-out-of-five-year provision, you may want to delay the sale and move in until you do qualify.

What about claiming you lived there? As we all know, anything can be claimed. I suspect, however, that the Internal Revenue Service isn't likely to look favorably on a less-than-legitimate claim. If you have rented out the property for more than three years, you probably will be challenged as to whether or not you meet the requirement.

Other Rules

Other rules apply for people who are not married living in the home, who divorce, who file separately, who previously used the property as an investment and used a Section 1031 tax-deferred exchange on it, and on and on. Check with a good tax professional for full information.

Should I Watch the Time Frame Closely?

If you anticipate selling your home FSBO in the near future, it would be wise to spend some time with a tax consultant to determine the optimum time for selling. It might turn out that you don't qualify for the exclusion noted above because you haven't lived in the home two out of the previous five years. In that case, maybe you'd want to live there a while longer to be sure that you qualify.

Further, you'll want to determine what, if any, your capital gain will be. (After all, if it's a tiny amount, you may not care if you have to pay taxes on it.) The capital gains calculation requires that you apply a fairly rigorous set of calculations to the monies you anticipate from the sale. It could turn out, for example, that after improvements to the property that you've made are added in, you have little to no capital gain. Or if your property is in a rapidly appreciating area, perhaps the gain is huge. Depending on the calculation and the time frame, you may want to hold off on the sale—or move forward with it even more rapidly!

If the Gain Is Much Higher Than the Exclusion, Can Part of It Be Rolled Over?

The exclusions rule is great if you don't make too much money on the sale of your home. But it's not so great for those relatively few homeowners who have huge profits.

In the old days (before the 1997 law went into effect), you could "roll over," or defer, the payment of capital gains taxes, provided you bought a replacement house within two years and fulfilled other requirements. The amount you could roll over was unlimited.

However, the new law did away with the rollover provision. If your gain is more than the maximum exclusion, then you must pay tax on everything above the limit. You can't roll the excess over into a replacement home.

The Exclusion Applies Only to Your Capital Gain

This is an important point, because many sellers confuse what they consider profit with a capital gain. *Capital gain* is a very specific figure that must be determined in a manner prescribed by the tax code, which is enforced by the Internal Revenue Service.

Your capital gain is basically the sales price less most costs of sale less your basis in the property (usually what you paid for it plus improvements and other items and minus depreciation, if any, and other items). In other words, if you paid $100,000 including costs for the property, that is probably your basis. If you later sell for $150,000 after most costs of sale, your capital gain will be around $50,000.

Sounds simple?

Sometimes it is; sometimes it isn't. As noted earlier, I would strongly suggest that unless you're very familiar with the tax code, you do not try to determine your capital gain yourself. It's worth the few dollars required to have a CPA do it right.

What Happened to the Once-in-a-Lifetime Exclusion for Those Aged 55 and Older?

Under the old rules, you were allowed to exclude up to $125,000 once in a lifetime after age 55, provided other conditions were met. The new up-to-$250,000/$500,000 exclusion does away with the old rule. You can take the new exclusion every two years as many times as you want (providing you meet the two-out-of-five-year minimum stay requirement). You can take it at any age. You no longer must wait until you're 55.

Do State Laws Reflect the Federal Tax Code?

It's important to understand that the federal tax code only applies to federal income tax. Each state decides whether to reflect the federal code or go its own way.

Most states have reworked their tax codes to match or at least be similar to the federal tax code. However, don't assume that what works for the feds will automatically work for the state. You may be responsible for taxes under two sets of tax codes (federal and state). You might be able to exclude at the federal level but still owe taxes (or perhaps be able to roll them over) at the state level. Be sure to consult your accountant.

What If I Have an Office in My Home?

You may be able to get a deduction for it. There are many rules, however, to follow.

For example, the space allocated for office use must be used *exclusively* for business purposes. Further, the business must actually be viable (not just a hobby). In other words, at some point, you have to make a profit.

There are many other requirements for a home office. And there are many consequences as well.

For example, if you are using a portion of your home as an office at the time you sell, that portion may not fully qualify for the up to $250,000 exclusion. In other words, just like splitting up a duplex into a portion you lived in and a portion you rented out, you might have to split up the home as part residence and part business, and the business part may not qualify for the exclusion.

Further, if you took depreciation on your home office at some time in the past, you might be required to recapture that depreciation. In other words, the depreciation you took may now be taxed at a special rate.

Obviously, this entire subject of a home office is complex. Here again, be sure to consult a tax professional on your options and your tax liability if you've ever had an office in your home.

16 After You've Found a Buyer: Closing the Deal

EVERY BY-OWNER SELLER instinctively knows that the hardest part of selling their home is finding a buyer. Most figure if they can just get that buyer to sign on the dotted line, they've made it over the finish line.

In truth, however, it's not just finding a buyer that's critical—it's also closing the deal. All the work that's gone before can be wasted if the deal never closes. In this chapter, we're going to look at what you need to do to complete the sale.

The Closing Process

Once you've found a buyer and gotten a signed sales agreement, it normally takes anywhere from 30 to 90 days to close. Along the way, you could have a lot of problems to solve and tasks to perform. Here's how a typical 30-day escrow might run.

Steps in the Closing Process

(30-Day Escrow)

First week:
- Sales agreement is signed, buyer gets disclosures.
- Buyer applies for mortgage.
- Escrow is opened and deposit inserted.

Second Week:
- Check with lender on mortgage application process.
- Title search is completed.
- Inspections are ordered.

Third Week:
- Termite work and other repairs are done.
- Title problems, if any, are cleared.
- Lender gives buyer formal loan approval.

Fourth Week:
- Buyer does final walk-through.
- Buyer signs loan documents.
- Seller signs off on title.
- Deal closes.

What to Do the First Week

The closing process begins when you get a signed sales agreement. As soon as that's done (see chapter 13), you'll want to open escrow.

Open Escrow

Most states now use escrow services for real estate transactions. These, however, can be handled not only by an independent escrow company but also by an attorney. This latter is often done on the East Coast, where attorneys regularly handle closings.

Opening escrow means that you take your signed sales agreement to the escrow officer and receive an escrow number.

You will also need to contact a title company so that the buyer can be given clear title to your property. Most escrow companies work in conjunction with title insurance companies.

The title company now begins a title search to be sure that you can give the buyer clear title to your property. The escrow company itself will draw up all the documents (with the exception of the loan documents, which will come from the lender) needed to complete the transaction.

Because this all takes time, you want to open escrow immediately after signing the sales agreement.

Also, you will want to put the deposit money the buyer gave you into escrow. As noted earlier, the buyer is unlikely to trust you with this money. The easiest solution to this potential problem is to have the check made out to escrow, an independent third party.

Keep in mind, however, that if the deal doesn't go through and no language specifies what is to happen to the deposit in that event (see your attorney about this when creating the sale agreement), the money will remain in escrow. It will go to neither you nor the buyer until you both agree on its disposition. I've seen a deposit languish for months in escrow while the buyer and seller argued over who was to get what. It's best that you have your attorney write language about this beforehand.

Be Sure That the Buyer Applies for a Mortgage

This is critical because without a mortgage, you won't have a deal. (You may have a better chance of winning a state lottery than of finding an all-cash buyer.) Although you can't normally walk the buyers to a lender, you can insert a clause in the sales agreement specifying that the buyers will immediately apply for a mortgage and if the buyers aren't fully pre-approved, the lender will fully pre-approve them and issue a commitment within a reasonable amount of time, say 7–14 days from the signing of the sales agreement.

KEY CONCEPT *Full approval means that the lender has checked the buyers' credit, verified income and cash on hand, and determined the buyers will qualify for the needed mortgage. The lender may then issue a commitment letter. This is different from a preliminary pre-approval letter, which may not have gone through all of the above steps.*

You can check by phone with the buyers to find out which lender they have gone through and then check with that lender to see how the mortgage is progressing. (Note: Sometimes the lenders will not talk directly to you, only to the borrower.)

However, your safety valve is that final lender's commitment letter. If you don't get it within the specified 7–14 days, you may want to return the buyers' deposit and start looking for a new buyer. (In the past, it often took a full 30 days to get such a commitment from a lender, but today with electronic processing, the time is usually much shorter.)

Why be so strict?

The reason for being strict here is that in 99 cases out of 100, what makes the deal go through (title changes hands and you get your money) is having buyers who can get the necessary mortgage.

But what about that pre-approval letter that the buyer initially showed up with?

Unfortunately, even with a pre-approval letter that you receive before you signed the purchase agreement, you don't know for sure that buyers will be approved for a new mortgage. I have worked with buyers who, seemingly, had excellent credit, only to find weeks into the deal that they had hidden a foreclosure or a bankruptcy or bad payments in another state. In one case, a buyer seemed to have enormous income; only later did it come out that he had to make huge alimony and child support payments, which reduced the amount of his income that could be applied to the mortgage and disqualified him.

What to Do the Second Week

The approval/commitment letter of the buyer for a mortgage should have been issued. If it hasn't, you need to find out why not. It might turn out that your buyer can't qualify.

If the letter has been issued, don't relax yet. Many things could happen between now and the time title changes hands to cause the loan not to fund. For example, the buyer could lose her job. Or maybe the buyer will spend the down payment money elsewhere. Even the lender could go out of business!

 KEY CONCEPT *A good rule of thumb is to not count on the deal's closing until it's closed!*

Get the Preliminary Title Report

This should be issued by the second week by the title company you're using. It will reveal any problems you may have on your title.

Don't smirk. You may have problems you don't even know about. For example, someone may have filed a lien on your property in error. You may be totally innocent, but now you have to locate whoever filed that lien, convince that party of the error, and have it removed. Sometimes you have to get an attorney to accomplish this.

Other problems could affect the title, such as an encumbrance or easement that prevents you from getting clear title. It's up to you to identify the problem and solve it.

Order Inspections

Another matter is the various inspections that may be needed. The buyer will need to order a professional home inspection, but you'll want to track this to be sure it's done. (Usually the buyer will pay for the professional home inspection at the time it is done.) Also, you will need to coordinate any buyer's inspections so that the property is available to be seen when the inspector arrives.

Almost certainly, the lender will require a termite clearance before funding the loan. This you will typically need to order. To get a termite clearance, you (not the buyer) need to order a termite inspection.

Note that if for some reason the sale doesn't close, you will be responsible for paying for the costs of any inspections you order. That is why I suggest waiting a week to see if the buyer gets that letter of commitment from the lender. At least then you have a better hope that the deal will close.

What to Do the Third Week

By the third week you should be really rolling. The inspections should have been done and any required repairs noted. In addition, any credit problems the buyer has should have surfaced. If none has, the lender will set a date for funding the loan. This means that your buyer has the mortgage in the bag. (But be careful: as we'll see shortly, that bag could still have a few holes in it.)

Once the buyer has final loan approval (or earlier, as needed), you will want to authorize repair work. (You authorize it because usually you're paying for it.) This may mean anything from fixing a broken window to tenting the house to remove termites. Just keep in mind that once the work is ordered, it must be paid for whether or not the deal closes. For that reason, most sellers wait until the last possible moment before ordering the work done.

Finally, you should have cleared up any problems in the title, removing any mistaken liens and other title clouds.

What to Do Your Fourth Week

By the fourth week in an ideal closing, the lender is ready to fund. The buyer may want a final walk-through. (See below for more details.) Here the buyer again looks at the house, hopefully just to see that it's in the same condition as when the sales agreement was signed.

Once the final walk-through is completed, the buyer will go to the escrow officer and sign all the loan documents, as well as deposit the cash down payment and closing costs. The escrow officer will let you know when this has to be done. (Lenders usually leave a window of only a few days during which all the documents must be finalized.)

Once the buyer has signed the documents, you need to sign the deed, as well as any additional escrow instructions.

And then you're done!

Now you wait.

You are waiting for the lender to fund the loan, then for the escrow officer to record the deed and mortgage and issue your check to you. If the deed is recorded in the morning, you can usually have your check the same day.

What If Problems Arise?

As the famed baseball star Yogi Berra was fond of saying, "It ain't over 'til it's over."

What could possibly go wrong? Probably very little, but there's always something. The lender might not fund. The lender might have discovered a credit or income problem with your buyer at the 11th hour—unlikely, but it could happen—or the lender might itself suddenly be immersed in financial problems and not have the funds needed. Also, someone might record a lien or other encumbrance affecting your title. Again it's unlikely, but it could happen.

If the unforeseen does happen, you'll simply have to deal with it. In most cases, the worst that will happen is a delay. It is possible, however, in a worst-case scenario, to lose the deal after everything is signed and before the deed has been recorded.

Longer Closings

What we've seen here is an ideal 30-day closing. Yours may take much longer. The need for extensive physical repairs may prolong the escrow, a title problem could require an attorney and court action to eliminate, the buyer may not be able to get all the cash together immediately, or anything else could happen. These days, escrows of 60 and even 90 days are not uncommon.

Beware, however, of the buyers losing their loan in a longer-than-anticipated escrow. Lenders often offer commitments to fund. This means that the lender guarantees a rate and points for a specified time. That time, however, is rarely more than 45 days and usually is just 30 days. If the escrow takes longer, the lender may still fund but not at the originally quoted interest rate or points. That means the buyers might not qualify.

Also, if interest rates have jumped up after the sales agreement was signed but before the escrow closes, it could cost your buyer more money and higher payments. She may not want or be able to pay more. Depending on how the sales agreement was prepared, your buyer may be able to walk if interest rates rise above a ceiling (which is a good reason to specify a higher-than-current rate for interest and points for the buyer in the sales agreement). Or the lender may say that your buyer qualified at a lower rate but not at the newer, higher rate.

No, it's not likely to happen, but a longer escrow can bring its own set of problems. If I have the option, I always go for the shortest escrow possible.

Closing-the-Deal Checklist

☐ Open escrow: use the signed sales agreement to open escrow and place buyer's deposit in it.

☐ Be sure buyer applies for mortgage.

☐ Check on that approval/commitment letter.

☐ Order inspections.

☐ Remove any title problems you may have.

☐ Check on buyer's progress in getting mortgage.

☐ Find out when mortgage will fund.

☐ Order all repair work that needs to be done.

☐ Do final walk-through.

☐ Sign all documents.

The Final Walk-Through

It has become common practice to offer buyers an opportunity to have a final look at the property just before closing escrow. This final walk-through often takes place immediately before the buyers go to the escrow office and sign their loan documents and deliver their cash down payment and closing costs. The purpose is to allow buyers to confirm that the property is in the same shape as it was when they first saw it and that any agreed-upon repairs have, in fact, been properly done.

Why Allow a Final Walk-Through?

Most sellers look at the final walk-through as a pain in the you-know-where. They see it as, at best, an opportunity for the buyers to nitpick and demand more things be done and, at worst, as an opportunity for the buyers to back out of the deal.

It can be both of those things, if not properly controlled. However, the real reason for having a final walk-through is to avoid serious problems *after* the sale is completed. It is based on the belief that "a stitch in time saves nine." If you can discover a problem before the sale is completed, you have a much better chance of solving it cheaply and effectively than if its found afterward.

What Sort of Problems Can Arise?

Problems can be almost anything. For example, say one of the conditions of sale is that you replace a bathroom floor because it was moldy. You've done it. But the buyers thought it would be replaced with tile, and you've replaced it with less-expensive linoleum. They are very unhappy.

If this discovery happens after the sale, the buyers may be faced with living with linoleum or suing you. Some choose the latter course, which is a big problem for you. (Even if you win a lawsuit, your attorney's fees can be staggering. If it goes to small claims court where no lawyers are involved, the judges often exercise a Solomon-like discretion, splitting the decision between parties.)

On the other hand, if the discovery is made prior to closing the sale, you have an opportunity to deal with it directly. You still have possession (presumably) of the home. You can go back and put in tile. (You can even do it yourself at a nominal cost.) Or you can make a money concession to the buyers. Or... In other words, you can come up with a solution that works, that is inexpensive, and that avoids later unpleasantness.

The types of problems that occur are many and sometimes very surprising. Here are some of the problems I've encountered at a final walk-though.

Changed Fixture. Buyers claim that a chandelier (or other light fixture) was not the same one they originally saw. You changed out the fixtures.

If you're going to switch fixtures, do it *before* you begin showing your home to prospective buyers. Otherwise, the buyers will assume everything they see goes with the house. You can, of course, try to exclude items in the purchase agreement, but that's likely to produce a fight. What the buyers don't see, they won't want.

Buyers Dislike Repair Work.

They claim that agreed-upon work was not done, was not done in a workmanlike manner, or the wrong materials were used.

Go back to the original purchase agreement and see what it says. It may turn out that you have discretion about what to do, how to do it, and when to do it. If the buyers signed, then they are committed to move forward regardless. Inform them of the penalties (loss of deposit and a possible lawsuit) for failing to complete the transaction as agreed. On the other hand, if you agreed to do something and haven't done it, get it done. Else you could face the same penalties!

Buyers Claim the House Is Dirty.

Buyers have a right to expect a reasonably clean home delivered to them. (You didn't recently throw an orgy, did you?!) However, at a final walk-through, you may have already removed your furniture, and when that happens, scratch marks on walls and floors that were hidden by the furniture almost always show up. Point out to the buyers that you never intended to repaint or scrub down the house. On the other hand, if you've thrown a few parties since the deal was made and haven't cleaned up after yourself, do it now.

Buyers Claim Something Is Broken That Was Working Before.

Normally, you agree to deliver the property in good condition, as it was when you first showed it to the buyers. That usually means, unless excluded, no broken windows or screens, all appliances working, heater and air conditioner working, and so forth. If something is broken, you will need to fix it.

Buyers Nitpick and Say They Want to Back Out of the Deal.

This is the most serious problem you can face at a final walk-though, and we'll deal with it at length.

When the Buyer Wants to Back Out

Why, you may ask yourself, would a buyer want to back out of the deal, particularly so late in the transaction process?

There can be many reasons:

- I've seen buyers who, at the last minute, found another property they preferred. They desired to back out of the deal to get the other home.
- In other cases, buyers simply never looked closely at the property. Now, when they are finally faced with the purchase and the need to move in, they discover they don't like it and want out.
- Sometimes buyers now take a good look at the neighborhood for the first time and decide that it's not what they want.
- The buyers could have financial problems. Perhaps some money they were expecting didn't show up, and they are afraid of committing to a big home purchase. Or maybe they have discovered a great investment opportunity and would rather put the money into that than into buying your house.
- Maybe you've made all sorts of changes to the house, and they don't like what you've done.

Regardless, all but the last reason given above are not acceptable. (If you've messed up by changing the house, you might lose the deal or might need to bring the house back to its original condition.)

When the buyers signed the purchase agreement, they committed to completing the transaction. It doesn't matter if they change their minds, a better investment shows up, or they find a more suitable house. They are committed to going through with the deal. However, converting that commitment into actually getting them to move forward can be a difficult thing.

What Does the Purchase Agreement Say?

It all goes back to what you and the buyers originally agreed to. Usually a purchase agreement will specify that the buyers have the right to conduct a final walk-through. But the devil is in the details. What are the specifics of this right?

(This is another reason you want an attorney or a good real estate agent to draw up the purchase agreement!)

Is Approval of the Walk-Through a Contingency of the Sale?

In some purchase agreements, the language is something to the effect that buyers must give approval of a final walk-through. What this is saying is that the purchase is contingent on the buyers' approval. If the buyers don't approve, there is no purchase. If language like this is in your purchase contract, then the buyers may indeed have a way out, regardless of their motives.

On the other hand, some purchase agreements say that the buyers will have an opportunity to have a final walk-through for the purpose of inspecting work that was done and determining that the home is essentially the same as it was when they first saw it. Some also add a notice that specifically states the final walk-through is not for the purpose of giving the buyers a new opportunity to decide whether or not to purchase.

This type of language makes it more difficult for buyers to back out of the deal. The only arguments here should be over how work was done and whether there were any significant changes to the property between the time the buyers first made their offer and the walk-through.

These are usually demonstrable sorts of things and can be settled, as noted earlier, by redoing work, by cleaning, or by replacing items. In other words, it should be possible to satisfy any of the buyer's reasonable demands and demonstrate that any unreasonable demands are, well, unreasonable.

Here, buyers who want to back out for hidden motives are faced with dealing with an angry seller, who might just keep their deposit and even take them to court for "specific performance" (forcing them to complete the purchase).

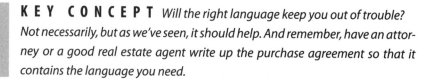

KEY CONCEPT *Will the right language keep you out of trouble? Not necessarily, but as we've seen, it should help. And remember, have an attorney or a good real estate agent write up the purchase agreement so that it contains the language you need.*

How Much Should You Bend?

We've seen two extremes. In one case, the buyers were justified in their demands made after the final walk-through. In the other, they were not.

But sometimes there's a gray area in between. For example, you agree to replace a rotting deck. You do the work and then stain the wood a redwood color.

The buyers come for the final walk-through and are dismayed. They wanted it to be a light cedar stain. They want you to change the color.

Changing the stain on wood is not so easy. After all, stain goes into the wood. To change could mean sanding down the wood or even replacing it and staining again—not something you'll want to do.

So what's to be done here?

If it were me and the buyers had, indeed, reasonably conveyed to me the color they wanted and I had forgotten or got it wrong, I would make a money concession. Perhaps knock a few hundred dollars off the price. Explain to the buyers that by next year, with the sun bleaching it, the wood will need restaining anyhow, and then they can get the cedar color they want. They might not be entirely satisfied, but it's a reasonable concession and they will most likely accept it.

On the other hand, if the buyers never expressed any color preference, and particularly if the previous deck was redwood stained, I would make no concession whatsoever. I would stick to my guns, note that the new deck was stained the same as the old, and demand the buyers continue with the purchase. More than likely they would, although again they might not be happy about it.

Only if this became such an incredibly big issue that the buyers were willing to risk losing their deposit and a possible lawsuit would I consider a concession, just to complete the transaction. And then only a small one! I might simply say, "Okay, I don't owe it, but here's a hundred bucks and let's finish the deal." Sometimes people just want to be right, and it's easier to let them have their way than to get into a legal hassle.

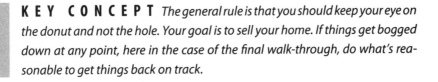

KEY CONCEPT *The general rule is that you should keep your eye on the donut and not the hole. Your goal is to sell your home. If things get bogged down at any point, here in the case of the final walk-through, do what's reasonable to get things back on track.*

17 Have You Considered a FSBO Auction?

EVERY TIME THAT housing prices take a dip, home auctions come into vogue. Have you seen advertisements for auctions in your area? They're happening all around the country.

In the minds of many, auctions are only for selling top-quality items, such as paintings, jewelry, rare coins, and so forth. Why, then, are they used for selling homes in a down market?

The answer is that because homes are so expensive, hence valuable, the techniques used at auctions can sometimes be applied to attract buyers and to get them to bid up prices. When the market's red-hot, you can see this happen informally when bidding wars occur over homes. In a down market, something similar sometimes can be made to happen in the more formal venue of an actual auction.

The key to any auction, of course, is that buyers must think they have the possibility of getting a bargain. That's what draws them in. However, once there, the excitement and the lure of getting a "deal" often makes people pay more than they otherwise would.

Of course, the beauty of an auction is that as a FSBO seller, you may be able to hold one yourself! (Or, you could sign up with one of the money auction companies, but be prepared to pay a stiff fee, possibly as high as a full commission.)

It's not the sort of thing that most people think about doing. Yet if handled correctly, and if there's enough publicity, you can use the technique to get rid of an otherwise hard-to-sell property. (In rare cases, you can even get an above-market price for it!)

A home auction is just what it sounds like. You get people to bid on your property until the winning bid buys the home, hopefully at a price you want to sell it for.

Sound simple? It is. On the other hand, there are many pitfalls. Selling a *single* home at auction can be one of the most difficult auctioneering tasks. Here are the pros and cons. (Be sure to check the end of this chapter for possible restrictions on holding an auction in your area.)

Pros of Auctioning Off Your House

There are basically three reasons to auction your home:

1. *You want a quick sale.* The entire auction process can take as little time as a few weeks. It's an excellent way to get out of your home fast.
2. *You have a hard-to-sell home.* Perhaps you've tried to sell FSBO and been unsuccessful. Maybe you've tried to sell by listing with an agent and also been unsuccessful. Your last, best hope now becomes the auction.
3. *The timing is right.* Home auctions work best in two kinds of markets—very slow and very hot. In a slow market, people come by hoping to get a steal. In a hot market, people come by because there are few homes in the housing inventory and they hope to get one.

How an Auction Works

You've probably been to or at least seen an auction at one time or another. The usual image most of us have is of a crowd of people sitting in a room (or under a tent) with an auctioneer at a lectern in front describing various "lots" for sale and banging down a gavel when the successful bidder wins.

That's the traditional auction. Indeed, auction companies often handle a home auction in exactly the same way, *if* they have a group of homes to dispose of. They will offer a period of time for viewing the home. They will provide an arena for the auction. And then a professional auctioneer will sell off the properties.

As noted, that works well when you have many properties to sell. A kind of fever builds at such times, and a skillful auctioneer can often get a better price for the homes than the market may warrant.

However, you presumably have only one home if you are going to do it yourself. So I suggest a "silent" auction. Here buyers make silent bids for the property during an open auction period. Bidders can either see other bids as in an open auction, or the bids can be sealed as in a closed auction. When the auction period ends, the bids are all opened, and the winner gets the house.

No, it's not quite that simple, as we'll see.

Cons of Auctioning Off Your Home

To pull off a successful auction yourself, you will need to jump a series of hurdles. Here's a list of some of them:

- *Handling the paperwork.* This includes the auction documents as well as the usual purchase agreement and other documents.
- *Getting publicity.* An auction will only work if lots of people know about it. Usually they have to learn of it quickly, just before the auction is held. You have to find a way to get the word out.
- *Qualifying bidders.* You need to qualify bidders, otherwise anyone can make a bid, even the neighborhood cat!
- *Deciding whether to hold an "absolute" or a "reserve" auction. Absolute* means that no matter how low the winning bid, you'll still sell the house. Holding a *reserve* means that there's a minimum price below which you won't go.
- *Conducting the actual auction.* Someone has to conduct it, and you know who that's going to be!
- *Closing the sale.* Handling the financing, escrow, inspections, disclosures, and so on. And then, what do you do if the top bidder either backs out or fails to get a mortgage?

Let's consider some of the essential concerns of holding an auction in more detail. A closer look may help you to decide if it's something you're really interested in.

How Do I Handle the Paperwork?

This should be fairly straightforward with the information from this book. For the usual work, you can look for a real estate agent who can handle the purchase agreement and other documentation and, if possible, hire that person for a fee, which you can negotiate.

There will, however, be some additional paperwork, namely the documentation that spells out the terms of the auction. This needs to be done correctly so you don't get into legal trouble later on (such as if there's no defined process for determining who's the winner with two identical bids). A good attorney, hopefully one who's handled auctions before, can be invaluable. Try to negotiate a set fee for doing all the paperwork with the attorney too.

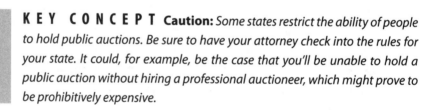

K E Y   C O N C E P T **Caution:** *Some states restrict the ability of people to hold public auctions. Be sure to have your attorney check into the rules for your state. It could, for example, be the case that you'll be unable to hold a public auction without hiring a professional auctioneer, which might prove to be prohibitively expensive.*

How Do I Handle the Publicity?

People are much more inclined to want to read about an auction than a simple house for sale. The word *auction* implies getting a bargain, and people are always up for bargains.

Therefore, I suggest you use the usual methods mentioned in this book, only emphasize the words "house auction" in addition to "by owner" in your advertising. Use the Internet, and try including such sites as Owners.com and Craigs list.com. (If you use eBay.com, you'll have to follow that site's procedures.)

Also, consider advertising in the local newspapers, putting out flyers (where allowed to do so), and putting a big sign on the property and even consider buying some low-cost spots on the local cable channel. If there's a major thoroughfare nearby, ask (or offer to pay a nominal sum to) a neighbor if you can place an auction sign on his lawn for a week. Many people are quite amenable to doing this, although some aren't.

It's critical that you get the word out to as many people as possible. The more who learn of the auction, the more who are likely to bid.

 K E Y   C O N C E P T *While being sure your advertisements contain enough information to whet the appetite of potential bidders, be sure they also contain enough disclaimers to protect you. Your attorney can help you with this.*

How Do I Qualify Buyers?

This is a huge problem. You want as many bidders as possible. On the other hand, you want to be sure that the bidders you get are sincere and can afford the property. How do you accomplish this?

One method is to have a fee for bidding. The fee need not be large, say only $50, and it should be fully refundable if the bidder is unsuccessful. Nevertheless, asking a person to put up some money up front often shakes out the wheat from the chaff. Only serious bidders will usually apply.

 K E Y   C O N C E P T *Some states prohibit accepting advance deposits or deposits that are not fully refundable. Check out the laws in your area.*

Further, you can insist that to obtain a bidding form (described below) the bidder must show that she has a deposit of a certain amount (typically $1,000 to $5,000) ready to give to you. They don't actually give the money to you; they just show that they have it, usually in the form of a cashier's check made out to an escrow company.

Additionally, you can insist that in order to bid, the bidders provide a pre-approval letter from a lender. As we saw in chapter 14, these are easy to get and are commonplace today. The letter should state, at minimum, the size of a mortgage the bidder can qualify for. You can immediately tell if it's big enough.

Of course, there's the matter of the bidder coming up with enough money to handle the down payment and the closing costs. Usually this is handled at the time of choosing the winning bid. For example, you can give the winning bidder a short period of time (24–72 hours) to come up with verification of enough money to close the deal. This is in addition to the deposit already described.

If the winning bidder can't do it, then you move down to the next bidder. (This is why you need expert help in creating your documentation—it must specify exactly what's to happen in this eventuality.)

Should I Sell Open or Closed? Absolute or with a Reserve?

In an open sale, each bidder can see how high the previous bid was. This encourages bidders to move the price up. However, the bidders can also see if there are few to no bids and if they are low. That discourages them from bidding or encourages low-ball bids.

If the sale is closed, the bidders have no idea how many other bids there are or what they are. This encourages people to make bids. However, there is no impetus to beat out other people; hence, the bidding may be disappointingly low.

Open or closed? There are arguments on both sides, and you have to decide which to use in your locale.

As for setting up your auction as absolute or with a reserve, for most people, this is an easy call. Put a reserve in, lest you sell your house for too little. Remember, a reserve is a minimum price below which you will not sell. It's only self-protection.

Yes, but...if you put a reserve in, you must disclose that you have a reserve to all potential bidders. Most people will just assume that you've put your reserve at or close to market price and, hence, there's no real "steal" to be obtained. Thus, putting in a reserve discourages bidding.

On the other hand, advertise that this is an absolute sale, and you'll have people coming from all over to bid. *Absolute* means that the top bid wins, no matter how low it may be. Everyone will want to enter a bid in the hopes of getting something for nothing. You'll get oodles of bids. Unfortunately, most may be very low.

Combining an absolute sale with an open bidding process often results in the highest bids. Unfortunately, it's also the riskiest and I don't advise it.

KEY CONCEPT *Remember, if the sale is absolute, you must sell to the highest bidder, even if that bid is for only $100!*

How Do I Handle the Actual Auction? (Silent)

Usually there's an auction period. It could be a few hours, a day, a few days, or even a few weeks. During the designated period, bidders are allowed to make their bids.

Usually, the bid must be on a prescribed form, which your attorney will provide, that is appropriate for your state. It may include a standard purchase agreement properly drawn up. Since most auctions are for cash to the seller, it is assumed that the buyer will have enough money for a down payment and will also get a new mortgage. This can be spelled out. You collect the bids, which usually can be changed or cancelled prior to the close of the auction.

At a given time and place, all the bids are opened and compared, and a winner is announced. Often there's a provision that the winning bidder must then give you a deposit typically in the form of a cashier's check (usually made out to an escrow company), for a minimum amount, perhaps $1,000 to $5,000. As noted, the winner may have a minimum amount of time to do this. The purpose is to cement the sale, and this money is the equivalent of the normal deposit found in any real estate transaction.

If the winning bidder can't quickly produce the cashier's check, the bid is voided, and the next highest bidder selected.

Once the winning bidder is announced and produces the appropriate deposit, you conclude the sale by filling out and signing a purchase agreement (usually handled by an agent or attorney) in the usual manner.

And you've sold your home! (Hopefully for a high price!)

How Do I Handle the Closing?

The closing is handled in the usual way, as described in chapter 16. The auction process is just used to produce a buyer. Once you have a buyer, everything else proceeds as usual.

The one exception is that with an auction, you usually also have backup buyers: all those unsuccessful bidders. This is useful in keeping pressure on the winning bidder to keep things moving along. He realizes that if he doesn't financially perform, you have other buyers waiting in the wings.

 K E Y   C O N C E P T *Don't count on those other buyers. They may have long since forgotten about the auction or have purchased other properties. Their existence is nice to keep the pressure on the winning bidder, but they may not be there if you actually need them.*

What About Government Restrictions?

Each state handles auctions a little differently. Some are very strict, requiring that the process be handled exclusively by a licensed professional. Others are more laid-back and don't seem to care much at all. Most, however, are quite specific about saying that you must reveal whether the auction is absolute or reserved.

Be sure to check with a professional in your state before conducting your auction to be sure you're in compliance with all rules and laws.

Can I Really Do It?

You certainly can give it a try. Success will depend on your ingenuity, carefulness, and some daring.

18 What Do I Do If My Home Just Won't Sell?

SOMETIMES, IN SPITE of our best efforts, homes don't sell. You put your house up for sale by FSBO, and after a month, two months, maybe even three months or more, it still hasn't sold. What now?

If this happens to you, first and foremost, don't panic. It's time to get a cup of tea (or coffee), catch a deep breath, and reflect. It's time to look at your alternatives. In this chapter, we'll discuss what your options are.

By the way, if you're one of those anxious people who turned to this chapter first, stop. Don't bother reading here, because chances are you won't need this information. Go back to the beginning, keep an optimistic outlook, and get started selling your home by owner.

Typical Reasons a Home Doesn't Sell

Following are the top five reasons a home might not sell:

1. Resale market is bad.
2. Location is poor.
3. Price is too high.
4. House shows badly.
5. Financing isn't competitive.

If you've given a FSBO sale your best shot and your home still hasn't sold, then you have to look for likely causes. Let's consider each of the above five reasons separately.

Resale Market Is Bad

As of this writing, the residential resale market in most areas of the country is downright unhealthy. However, that certainly hasn't always been the case and will not always be the case in the future.

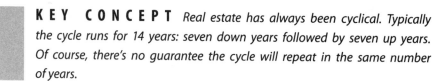

KEY CONCEPT *Real estate has always been cyclical. Typically the cycle runs for 14 years: seven down years followed by seven up years. Of course, there's no guarantee the cycle will repeat in the same number of years.*

If you can't sell, it may simply be that nothing at all is selling in your area. Check with an agent who belongs to the local real estate board to find out how many houses are selling per month in your area.

If it's next to none, you immediately know what your problem is—the market in your area is severely depressed. If that's the case, consider some of the alternatives given later in this chapter.

Your Home's Location Is Poor

Another reason for the inability to sell is a poor location. Factors making for a poor location include the following:

- A nearby environmental hazard, such as a dump site
- High-tension electrical wires overhead
- A sewer facility of some sort in close proximity
- A noisy or smelly factory next door
- Undesirable commercial usage (such as a gas station) next door
- A particularly high-crime area

- A blighted neighborhood
- Overly high density
- Narrow streets

While you may have taken location into account initially when you bought the property, perhaps you didn't give it enough weight. Regardless of how nice your particular house is, potential buyers may be shunning your area because of some nearby detrimental influence.

If this is the case, then the only realistic thing you can do is lower your price and/or offer more advantageous terms. If you had time, you could attempt to organize the neighborhood and seek ways to change the harmful influence, but that could take years. To attract buyers in the short run, you may simply have to make your house into more of a bargain.

Your Price Is Too High

Even if you don't have a bad neighborhood influence, your home may still be priced too high for the local market to bear. Perhaps you didn't do as good a job of checking comparables as you thought. Remember, while for you, checking the market is an academic exercise, for buyers it is an urgent and vital task.

After a few days of looking at homes, buyers become very attuned to what a house should sell for. If your home is even a few thousand over market price, they may shun it and not make offers.

Re-examine the comparables. For a weekend, pretend you're a buyer and visit every home for sale in your area. (Work with an agent on this.) Very quickly, you'll see if you've priced yourself even a little bit too high. (Remember, when the market's down, you have to get ahead of it by discounting your price.)

Then you'll have to suck in your breath, take the plunge, and lower your price accordingly.

Your House Shows Badly

Re-examine the appearance of your house, only don't take your own word on it. Seek the advice of experts. Contact two or three agents. (After having put your home up FSBO, you should have the names of dozens of agents who have contacted you.) Ask them to come in, and tell them that you've had trouble selling FSBO. You're thinking of listing (which you undoubtedly are). Would they have any suggestions to make about the outside/inside presentation of your home? What should you fix? What should you stage differently?

You may be astonished at the suggestions offered. It may turn out that the wonderful shrubs that you have grown lovingly over the years are hiding the front of your house and need to be hacked out. Maybe the entranceway that you painted lavender would look better in beige. Perhaps the tile you yourself laid in the front hall would be better if removed and linoleum professionally laid in its place.

The point here is that you probably aren't able to see objectively what's wrong with the presentation of your property. If two or three others, however, all agree on some item that needs to be improved, consider doing the work. Once it's done, try again to sell FSBO. Removing the objection may result in quickly hooking a buyer.

Your Terms Aren't Competitive

Although we've discussed this at length in chapter 14, sometimes it's hard to really believe it applies to you. In a tight market, sometimes you cannot easily sell for cash. Cash-down buyers may just not be out there. Hence, to get a sale, you may have to accept a low down payment and carry some of the paper yourself.

I know that getting cash out of your property is often the most advantageous method of selling. You know it too. But if your choice is to sell with paper or not to sell at all, what are you going to do? Sometimes you have to compromise.

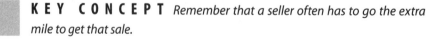 **KEY CONCEPT** *Remember that a seller often has to go the extra mile to get that sale.*

Your Other Alternatives

If you've considered the five main reasons for failure to sell noted above, have taken what corrective steps you can, and still can't sell your property, what are your alternatives now?

List with a Full-Service Broker

It may sound heretical, but my suggestion is that if you've done your best trying to sell by owner and you still can't find a buyer after a reasonable time, then consider listing with an agent. You can still list with a discount broker, as noted in chapter 10, or you can list with a full-service, full-commission broker.

Don't wedge yourself into a corner by stubbornness. Don't fail to sell simply because you can't do it FSBO.

The key, of course, is how much time you've given yourself. As I've noted in many places, set a reasonable time limit, whether it's a couple of months or half a year. If you still have not sold after the time has expired, consider listing.

Take It Off the Market

Maybe no houses are selling in your area. The market could be terrible—so terrible, in fact, that you simply can't find a buyer either FSBO or through an agent.

If that's the case, consider hanging onto your property until times get better, which they surely will. This means that you may have to hold your property for a year or more. Ideally, you will be able to continue living in your property, working in the area, and making the payments. If you can do all of this, then you may simply want to defer selling for a while. Remember, when the market eventually does turn up, you will probably be able to sell quickly and, very likely, for more money.

Rent It

Maybe you can't sell and you can't stay there. Perhaps you have to move because of a change in employment. Perhaps an illness requires you to get out from under that mortgage payment. If you can't stay and you can't sell, consider renting the property.

Very often, particularly if you've been there a few years, you can rent the property for at least your mortgage payment. And you may be able to write off your interest, taxes, insurance, and other costs as well as depreciation when you convert a personal residence to an investment property. That can actually give you a tax advantage at year-end.

K E Y   C O N C E P T *The tax rules may restrict your ability to write off any real estate losses against your personal income. Check with your accountant.*

Of course, renting out your property also carries risks. Tenants almost never treat the property as well as you would. There's bound to be some wear and tear in the best of situations, and if you get a bad tenant, there could be real damage. In a worst-case scenario, you might need to evict a tenant as well as refurbish your home. Of course, if you rent judiciously, you're less likely to face this situation. I suggest you check into *The Landlord's Troubleshooter* by my favorite author (Kaplan, 2004).

Try a Lease Option

Yet another alternative is the lease option. Here you lease the property to a tenant and, typically, allow a certain percentage of the higher rent payment to apply toward a down payment if the renter eventually purchases the home. You have combined leasing with the potential for purchase.

Lease options become more favored during slumping real estate markets. However, their value is directly related to the tenant's eventually exercising the option and purchasing the property. If the tenant doesn't eventually buy, you will take back the property, often in poor condition, because at the end of the lease option period, the tenant may resent the higher monthly payment and take it out on the property.

A lease option needs to be correctly drawn and executed, so you would be wise to pay an agent and attorney to draft one for you. Also, carefully screen the renter/buyer. You want someone who can make the payments and eventually buy the property (see also Chapter 14).

 KEY CONCEPT *Several states, including Texas, have restricted a seller's ability to use a lease option. Check with a good real estate agent or attorney in your area to see what rules apply to you.*

Walk Away

Bad choice. In desperate situations, some sellers who can't sell (they may owe more than their property is worth), can't stay (their job may require a move to a different state), and can't lease (too many properties are for rent or for sale) simply walk away from their properties. They let the house go into foreclosure.

I don't recommend this—ever. A foreclosure ruins your credit rating. Although you may be able to establish enough credit to get a credit card in a few years, it could take longer, if ever, before a lender is willing to give you another home mortgage.

If you are desperate, my suggestion is that you immediately call the mortgage lender to see whether it's possible to make an arrangement that would benefit both of you. Perhaps instead of foreclosure, you can simply give the lender a deed to your property. Called a "deed in lieu" of foreclosure, it will still adversely affect your credit but probably not as much as a foreclosure.

Keep in mind that lenders usually threaten to foreclose while hoping to pressure you into keeping up your payments. Have your attorney look into the possibility of bankruptcy for you. The threat of a personal bankruptcy holding up disposition of a home for months, perhaps years, often brings a reluctant lender around to your way of seeing things.

Figure 18.1 Checklist for When Your House Doesn't Sell

YES   NO

- ☐ ☐ 1. How is the general resale market in your area?
- ☐ ☐ 2. If it's bad, have you tried reducing your price?
- ☐ ☐ 3. Why not?
- ☐ ☐ 4. Do you have a bad location?
- ☐ ☐ 5. If yes, have you tried reducing your price?
- ☐ ☐ 6. Why not?
- ☐ ☐ 7. Have you rechecked comparables lately?
- ☐ ☐ 8. If your house is priced above market, have you reduced the price?
- ☐ ☐ 9. Why not?
- ☐ ☐ 10. Have you asked several agents about the appearance of your home?
- ☐ ☐ 11. If it shows badly, have you improved it?
- ☐ ☐ 12. Why not?
- ☐ ☐ 13. Are you offering seller-financed terms?
- ☐ ☐ 14. If not, why not?
- ☐ ☐ 15. Have you considered listing?
- ☐ ☐ 16. Why not?
- ☐ ☐ 17. Have you considered leasing?
- ☐ ☐ 18. What about a lease option?
- ☐ ☐ 19. If you're desperate, have you considered a deed in lieu of foreclosure?
- ☐ ☐ 20. Have you talked with an attorney?

Appendix: Seller's Disclosure Statement

THE FOLLOWING STATEMENT MAY NOT BE SUITABLE FOR USE IN YOUR STATE, LOCALE, OR TRANSACTION. TAKE IT TO A LOCAL ATTORNEY OR REAL ESTATE AGENT AND ASK HIM OR HER TO MAKE IT APPROPRIATE FOR YOUR STATE AND LOCALE AND FOR YOUR SPECIFIC TRANSACTION. SOME STATES AND THE FEDERAL GOVERNMENT REQUIRE SPECIAL ITEMS TO BE DISCLOSED AND/OR REPORTS GIVEN TO BUYERS WHICH ARE NOT INCLUDED HERE.

SELLER'S DISCLOSURE STATEMENT

(To be filled out by seller and given to buyer. Seller, use a separate page to explain any defects or problems with property.)

YES NO **WATER**

☐ ☐ Any leaks (now or before) in the roof?

☐ ☐ Around a skylight, at a chimney, door, window, or elsewhere?
Was the problem corrected?
How?
By whom?
When? _____ By permit? _____
Final inspection when? _____

☐ ☐ Does the house have gutters?
Condition? _____

☐ ☐ Does the house have downspouts?
Condition? _____

☐ ☐ Any drainage problems?
Explain _____
How corrected? _____

YES NO **WATER (continued)**

☐ ☐ Water directed away from house?

☐ ☐ Flooding or grading problems?

☐ ☐ Settling, slipping, sliding, or other kinds of soil problems?

☐ ☐ Any leaks at sinks, toilets, tubs, showers, or elsewhere in house?

☐ ☐ Public water? _____ Or well? _____
        Date well pump installed _____

☐ ☐ Low water pressure?

YES NO **TITLE**

☐ ☐ Are you involved in a bankruptcy?

☐ ☐ Are you in default on any mortgage?

☐ ☐ Do you currently occupy the property?

☐ ☐ Have you given anyone else an option lease or right of refusal on
        the property?

☐ ☐ Does the property have any bond liens?

☐ ☐ Can they be paid off without penalty?

☐ ☐ Are there any boundary disputes?

☐ ☐ Any encroachments or easements?

☐ ☐ Shared walls, fences, or other such areas?

☐ ☐ Any areas held in common such as pools, tennis courts, walkways,
        greenbelts, or other?

☐ ☐ Notices of abatement filed?

☐ ☐ Any lawsuits against seller that will affect title?

☐ ☐ Do you have a real estate license?

☐ ☐ Is there a homeowners association to which you must belong?

☐ ☐ Any current lawsuits involving the homeowners association?

☐ ☐ Any covenants, conditions, and restrictions in deed affecting
        property?

☐ ☐ Any easements or rights-of-way over property to public utilities or
        others?

☐ ☐ Have you received a copy of all the condominium/co-op
        documents?

YES NO **STRUCTURE**

☐ ☐ Any cracks in slab?

☐ ☐ Any cracks in interior walls?

☐ ☐ Any cracks in ceilings?

☐ ☐ Any cracks in exterior walls?

☐ ☐ Any cracks in foundation?

☐ ☐ Any driveway cracks?

☐ ☐ Any retaining walls?
       Cracked? _____ Leaning? _____ Broken? _____

☐ ☐ Any problems with fences?

☐ ☐ Is house insulated?
       Attic? _____ Walls? _____ Floor? _____

☐ ☐ Double-paned glass windows?

☐ ☐ Moisture barrier in areas below ground level?

☐ ☐ Sump pump?
       Where? _____ Why? _____

☐ ☐ Septic tank?
       Active? _____ Abandoned? _____ Filled? _____

☐ ☐ Connected to sewer?

YES NO **EQUIPMENT**

☐ ☐ Central furnace?
       Forced air? _____ Radiant/water? _____
       Radiant/electric? _____ Other? _____
       In working condition? _____

☐ ☐ Room heaters? In working condition? _____
       Type? _____
       Location? _____

☐ ☐ Central air conditioning?
       Installed date? _____ In working condition? _____

☐ ☐ Room air conditioners?
       Location? _____ In working condition? _____

☐ ☐ Furnace vented?

☐ ☐ Temperature relief valve on water heater?
       In working condition? _____

YES NO **EQUIPMENT (continued)**

☐ ☐ Spa?

☐ ☐ Pool?

☐ ☐ Pool heated?

☐ ☐ Cracks, leaks, or other problems with pool? Explain. _____

☐ ☐ Any aluminum wiring?

YES NO **HAZARDS AND VIOLATIONS**

☐ ☐ Any asbestos?

☐ ☐ Any environmental hazards including, but not limited to, radon gas, lead-based paint, storage tanks for diesel or other fuel, contaminants in soil or water, formaldehyde?

☐ ☐ Landfill on or near property?

☐ ☐ Is property in earthquake zone?

☐ ☐ Is property in flood-hazard zone?

☐ ☐ Is property in landslide area?

☐ ☐ Is property in high-fire-hazard area as described on a Federal Emergency Management Agency Flood Insurance Rate Map or a Flood Hazard Boundary Map?

☐ ☐ Is property in any special study zone that indicates a hazard or requires permission to add to or alter existing structure?

☐ ☐ Are there any zoning violations pertaining to property? (Explain separately.)

☐ ☐ Were any room additions built without appropriate permits? (Explain separately.)

☐ ☐ Was any work done to electrical, plumbing, gas, or other home systems without appropriate permit? (Explain separately.)

☐ ☐ Does the property have an energy conservation retrofit?

☐ ☐ Any odors caused by gas, toxic waste, agriculture, or other?

☐ ☐ Were pets kept on the property? Type? _____ Inside? _____

☐ ☐ Are there any pet odor problems?

☐ ☐ Are there any active springs on property?

☐ ☐ Any sinkholes on property?

☐ ☐ Is there any real estate development planned or pending in immediate area such as commercial, industrial, or residential development that could affect property values?

☐ ☐ Any abandoned septic tank?

☐ ☐ Is a Home Protection Plan available to the buyer?

YES NO **REPORTS THAT HAVE BEEN MADE**
The seller notes that the following reports have been made and are available to the buyer:

☐ ☐ Structural

☐ ☐ Geologic

☐ ☐ Roof

☐ ☐ Soil

☐ ☐ Sewer/septic

☐ ☐ Heating/air conditioning

☐ ☐ Electrical/plumbing

☐ ☐ Termite

☐ ☐ Pool/spa

☐ ☐ General home inspection

☐ ☐ Energy audit

☐ ☐ Radon test

☐ ☐ City inspection

YES NO **ITEMS THAT GO WITH THE PROPERTY**

☐ ☐ Window coverings

☐ ☐ Floor coverings

☐ ☐ Range

☐ ☐ Oven

☐ ☐ Microwave

☐ ☐ Dishwasher

☐ ☐ Trash compactor

YES   NO   **ITEMS THAT GO WITH THE PROPERTY** (continued)

☐   ☐   Garbage disposal

☐   ☐   Bottled water

☐   ☐   Burglar alarm system

☐   ☐   Gutters

☐   ☐   Fire alarm

☐   ☐   Intercom

☐   ☐   Electric washer/dryer hookups

☐   ☐   Sauna

☐   ☐   Pool

☐   ☐   Central heating

☐   ☐   Central air

☐   ☐   Central evaporative cooler

☐   ☐   Water softener

☐   ☐   Space heaters

☐   ☐   Solar heating

☐   ☐   Window air conditioners

☐   ☐   Sprinklers
        Where? _____

☐   ☐   Security gates

☐   ☐   Television antenna

☐   ☐   TV cable connections

☐   ☐   TV satellite dish

☐   ☐   Attached garage

☐   ☐   Detached garage

☐   ☐   Water heater Gas _____ Electric _____

☐   ☐   City water supply

☐   ☐   Public utility gas

☐   ☐   Propane gas

☐   ☐   Screens on windows

☐   ☐   Built-in barbecue

☐   ☐   Garage door opener number of remote controls _____

☐   ☐   Is the property equipped with smoke detectors?

YES NO **ITEMS THAT ARE SPECIFICALLY EXCLUDED FROM THE SALE**

☐   ☐   Window coverings _____

Where? _____

☐   ☐   Other Items

Explain. _____

☐   ☐   Lamps _____

Where? _____

SELLER IS AWARE OF THE FOLLOWING DEFECTS OR MALFUNCTIONS AND SPECIFICALLY DRAWS BUYER'S ATTENTION TO THEM:

BUYER IS ENCOURAGED TO MAKE A PHYSICAL INSPECTION OF THE PROPERTY AND TO EMPLOY THE SERVICES OF A COMPETENT INSPECTION COMPANY TO OBTAIN AN INDEPENDENT VERBAL AND WRITTEN REPORT OF THE PROPERTY'S CONDITION.

SIGNED BY SELLER AND BUYER

_____

_____

Index

Exclusive right-to-sell, 116-17, 119
Exclusivity arrangement, 114, 115

F
Facts, lack of, 4
Family photos, 63-64
Family room, 71-72
Fannie Mae, 197
Fantastic, 66
Fear, 5
Federal tax code, 214
FedEx Kinko's, 36
Fee-for-service agent/broker, 110, 115,
    123-28, 183, 184
  evaluating, 125-26
  locating, 125
  payment, 127
  reasons for, 127-28
  when pay, 128
Fiduciary relationship, 122-23
Final walk-through, 27, 224-26
Financing
  ad, 101-2
  cash, 202
Firm commitment pre-approval letter, 196-97
First mortgage, 206
Fix It, Stage It, Sell It, 57, 76
Fixer upper, 52, 65-66
Fixing up, 11, 54
Fixture changed, 225-26
Flat fee, 6-7, 25, 22
Flat-fee multiple listing service, 33, 91, 109-14
Flyers, 33, 36, 94-96
Foreclosure, 41, 201, 245
  alternatives to consider, 48-49
  causes of, 41-42
FSBO, 44-45
  future of, 49
  lender rapport, 45
  selling out, 43-44
  short sale, 45, 47-48
  understanding lender, 46-47
Forms, lack of, 4-5
Foundation damage, 170-71
Franchise, 136, 137
Freddie Mac, 197
Front door, 69
Full-service agent/broker, 111, 243
Furniture, 61-62
  staging, 74

G
Garage clutter, 62
Geller, Tom, 41
Great Depression, 5, 49

H
Half-commission rate, 118-19
Handyman special, 52
HelpUSell, 133
Hidden systems, 54
Home inspection, 26, 56, 171-75, 191, 221-22
  price renegotiation and, 175-76
  report, 161-64, 172
Home inspector, 56, 165-66
Home knowledge, 1-2, 9
Home office, 214-15
Home preparation, 6
Housing
  offices, 96
  value, 83-84

I
Income
  decline, 42
  verification, 194
Inconsistencies, 15
Independent broker, 136
Inducements, 98
Information box, 94-96
Interest-only mortgage, 43
Internet
  address, 35
  buyer, 145
Investment value, 81-82

J-K
Judicial foreclosure, 46
Kitchen, 75
  appliances, 66
  countertops, 66
Knowledge, 1-2, 9, 10

L
Landlord's Troubleshooter, The, 244
Late payments, 201
Leaking roof, 169-70
Lease option, 48, 206-7, 244-45
Legal services, 126, 129-30
Lender
  rapport, 45
  understanding, 46-47

Redeem your coupon for a listing on Owners.com – Free!

To help you get started marketing your home, with the purchase of *For Sale by Owner* we now include a listing on Owners.com—America's largest for sale by owner website.

Your listing includes:

- A professional webpage featuring all the details of your home
- Exposure to buyers searching on-line for homes in your area.
- Ability to upload photos and unlimited property description
- 24 hour toll-free answering service with private voicemail
- Personal email box for buyer inquiries
- Property featured through exclusive distribution partners
- Access to our sellers' forum and FSBO article library
- Flat Fee MLS available to reach the most qualified buyers

Here is your Owners.com listing certificate:

Owners.com Listing

To redeem your
Owners.com listing, go to:

http://www.owners.com/fsbokit

and enter your password:

ASFW2